DEMONSTRATING
RESULTS

*Using Outcome Measurement
in Your Library*

Rhea Joyce Rubin

for the

Public Library Association

AMERICAN LIBRARY ASSOCIATION

Chicago   2006

While extensive effort has gone into ensuring the reliability of information appearing in this book, the publisher makes no warranty, express or implied, on the accuracy or reliability of the information, and does not assume and hereby disclaims any liability to any person for any loss or damage caused by errors or omissions in this publication.

Composition by ALA Editions in Stempel Schneidler and Univers using QuarkXPress 5.0

Printed on 50-pound white offset, a pH-neutral stock, and bound in 10-point coated cover stock by McNaughton & Gunn

The paper used in this publication meets the minimum requirements of American National Standard for Information Sciences—Permanence of Paper for Printed Library Materials, ANSI Z39.48-1992. ∞

Library of Congress Cataloging-in-Publication Data

Rubin, Rhea Joyce.
 Demonstrating results : using outcome measurement in your library / Rhea Joyce Rubin for the Public Library Association.
  p.   cm. — (PLA results series)
 Includes bibliographical references and index.
 ISBN 0-8389-3560-5 (alk. paper)
 1. Library planning. 2. Library planning—United States. 3. Public libraries—Planning. 4. Public libraries—United States—Planning. 5. Public services (Libraries)—Evaluation. 6. Public services (Libraries) —United States—Evaluation. I. Public Library Association. II. Title. III. Series.
 Z678.R793 2006
 025.1—dc22   2005024218

Printed in the United States of America

10   09   08   07   06   5   4   3   2   1

To the memory of
Margaret E. Monroe,
adult services pioneer,
library educator,
and mentor,
1914–2004

Contents

Figures

Preface

I am often asked how I became involved in outcome measurement. The answer is not a simple one, because I have been moving toward it for many years.

I became a librarian because of my interest in how reading affects people, how it can lead to insights and help people transform their lives. As a child I saw that readers reacted differently to the same book, depending on their own situations. As a teen I saw how kids read for the vicarious experience. By the time I was thinking about college, I had decided to be a bibliotherapist, using books as tools for self-understanding and healing. My correspondence with Dr. Karl Menninger and with Ruth Tews, librarian at the Mayo Clinic, convinced me that librarianship was the road to take. With Dr. Margaret Monroe as my mentor, I studied bibliotherapy, but realized that it hadn't been a career option since its heyday in the 1930s. Even so, I knew that the underlying belief in the power of reading and book discussion was still valid. It was confirmed when, as a library school student, I worked in a mental hospital library; again in my first professional job as a jail librarian; and then again as an outreach librarian to residential facilities and isolated individuals in their homes.

In the past few years, as I've used outcome measurement in my evaluation work, I have come full circle back to how books and libraries help people make changes in their lives.

A number of years ago, the American Library Association had a slogan that I liked and adopted: "Libraries Change Lives." A colleague, explaining why she felt that the slogan was erroneous, reminded me that people make changes for themselves. She is right, of course. Library services and materials help them in their own efforts to change and grow. Outcome measurement can assess how well libraries do that.

Acknowledgments

I gratefully acknowledge the state library agencies of California, Massachusetts, and Connecticut, with whom I have worked on outcome measurement. Many workshop participants and LSTA grant applicants in those states have unknowingly helped me to write this book. My hat is off to all of you. Special thanks go to Liz Gibson, Carla Lehn, and Tom Andersen in California; Shelley Quezada and Beth Wade in Massachusetts; and Mary Engels in Connecticut.

Sandra Nelson, senior editor of the PLA Results Series, first conceived of this book and then ushered it into reality through her excellent editing and graphic skills. I also appreciate the contributions of June Garcia, associate editor of the Results Series, and members of the PLA Demonstrating Results Review Committee who critiqued drafts and made suggestions that have greatly improved this book: Jane Eickhoff of the Harford County Public Library (MD); Mary Engels of the Connecticut State Library; Susan Epstein, independent consultant; June Garcia, independent consultant; Danny Hales of the Suwannee River Regional Library (FL); Susan Paznekas of the Maryland Department of Education; Shelly Quezada of the Massachusetts Board of Library Commissioners; Rivkah Sass of the Omaha Public Library (NE); and Vicki Terbovich of the Maricopa County Library District (AZ).

I am especially indebted to Joan Durrance of the University of Michigan School of Information. Our discussions of evaluation and other library topics have been some of my best continuing education ever since "Let's Talk about It."

In a less direct way, my work has been guided by three wonderful librarian mentors: Ruth Tews of the Mayo Clinic, whose commitment to patient libraries convinced me to become a librarian; Margaret Monroe, whose work in library outreach and reading guidance inspired me in library school and beyond; and Kathleen Weibel, whose decision to start library service at the Cook County Jail—and to hire me to do so—set me on my slippery slope.

As always, special thanks go to my office staff: Lars on IT, Hannah on design, and Chip on entertainment and security.

Introduction

Managing a public library has always been hard work, and it is becoming even more difficult under the twin pressures of restricted public funding and rapid change. The Public Library Association (PLA) plays a major role in providing the tools and training required to "enhance the development and effectiveness of public librarians and public library services."[1] Since 1998, the PLA has provided support for the development of the Results Series, a family of management publications that are being used by library administrators, staff, and boards around the country to manage the libraries in their communities more effectively. The six publications in the Results Series that are available in 2006 are

The New Planning for Results: A Streamlined Approach[2]

Managing for Results: Effective Resource Allocation for Public Libraries[3]

Staffing for Results: A Guide to Working Smarter[4]

Creating Policies for Results: From Chaos to Clarity[5]

Technology for Results: Developing Service-Based Plans[6]

Demonstrating Results: Using Outcome Measurement in Your Library

In 2004, PLA executive director Greta Southard and the members of the PLA board made a long-term commitment to the Results Series. Sandra Nelson was selected to be senior editor of the series and June Garcia was asked to serve as associate editor. The PLA board authorized the funding required to publish five Results books between January 2005 and July 2007—approximately one every six months. This publication, *Demonstrating Results*, is the second of the five new publications. *Technology for Results* was published in mid-2005, and three additional titles are scheduled to be published over the next two years.

All of the Results Series publications—both current and proposed—provide a fully integrated approach to planning and resource allocation, an approach that is focused on creating change—on *results*. The underlying assumptions in each of the books are the same:

Excellence must be defined locally. It is a result of providing library services that match community needs, interests, and priorities.

Excellence does not require unlimited resources. It occurs when available resources are allocated in ways that support library priorities.

Excellence is a moving target. The best decision-making model is "estimate, implement, check, and adjust"—and then "implement, check, and adjust again."

Planning and Outcome Measurement

The foundation of the Results Series is *The New Planning for Results: A Streamlined Approach*. *The New Planning for Results* describes a library planning process that is focused on creating an actual blueprint for change rather than a beautifully printed plan for your office shelf. The process starts by looking at the community the library serves in order to identify what needs to happen to improve the quality of life for all of the community's residents. Once the community's needs have been established, library planners look for ways the library can collaborate with other government services and nonprofit agencies to help meet those needs. This, in turn, provides the information required to establish the library's service priorities.

The planning process includes significant participation by community residents who represent all of the constituencies served by the library: parents and children, working adults and seniors, businesspeople and civic leaders, students and educators, the various racial, ethnic, and religious groups in your community, government and nonprofit leaders, and all of the other groups that together create your unique community. By involving all of these groups in your planning process, you ensure that the services you provide are really what community residents want—and not what you or your staff or board think (or wish) that they want.

During the course of the planning process, community residents identify their visions for the future of their community. In essence, these vision statements describe the outcomes that community leaders hope will result in five to ten years from the combined efforts of the individuals, groups, and organizations that make up the community. As the planning process continues, the community vision statements are used to define library priorities. Finally, the library staff develop goals that reflect those priorities, and objectives to measure the progress toward reaching those goals.

Often during this process, the measures of success for a program or service shift from the vision statements of the community leaders to library-specific inputs and outputs. The community vision statement, "People who want employment will be able to find jobs," might end up being measured by the number of people who attend one or more job and career information programs. While this might seem to be a meaningful measure to the staff and board, most community members probably won't make the connection between the vision and the measure.

Library managers and boards are facing increasing pressure to justify library services in ways that go beyond the standard measures of circulation and program attendance. Both funders and taxpayers want to know what difference the programs and services that are funded with tax dollars make in the lives of the people who use those services. Outcome measurement provides the means to answer those questions. *Outcomes* are defined in the glossary of this book as "the benefits to the end user that demonstrate the effectiveness of a program or service. The benefits usually are changes in user knowledge, skills, behavior, attitude, or condition that may not have happened without the program or service."

To return to our example, the community vision statement "People who want employment will be able to find jobs," would be considered a community goal in the process described in this book (see figure 4 in chapter 1). The outcome statement for this community goal might be: "People who participate in the job and career program will find jobs." Library staff might develop this target for this outcome: "20 percent of the participants who attend all of the programs in the job and career series will get a job within one year of the end of the series." This makes the link between the services the library is providing and the community vision statement crystal clear to funders, taxpayers, staff, and program participants alike. You will read more about this example in chapter 3.

Although this book, like others in the Results Series, assumes that you have used the Planning for Results process to identify library priorities, that is not a prerequisite for using the processes and tools described here. In fact, this book is as likely to be used in libraries that have not developed plans as in those libraries that have. The Institute of Museum and Library Services (IMLS) requires that state library agencies include an outcome-based evaluation component in all direct grant programs for libraries and museums funded with Library Services and Technology Act (LSTA) monies.[7] This means that every library staff member who develops an application for an LSTA grant must consider outcome-based evaluation and be able to determine if the program in the application is suitable for outcome measurement. If the program is suitable for outcome measurement, the grant application must include an outcome measurement plan. The process for developing that plan is described in detail in this book.

Some Basic Definitions

Before you begin to read and use this book, it will be helpful if you understand how some basic terms have been used. Every public library is a little different. The staff in one library talk about "branches," in another library the term is "agencies," and in a third the staff refer to both branches and departments as "units." Some libraries have central libraries; others have main libraries. There are libraries that report to authority boards and libraries that are units of the government entity that funds them, which may or may not have advisory boards. These differences can cause confusion among readers because each reader expects to see his or her reality reflected in the terms and examples used. The following is a list of basic library terms and their meanings *in this book*:

> *Branch.* A separate facility.
>
> *Central library.* The largest library facility, normally in a downtown area; referred to as the main library in some places.
>
> *Department.* A unit within a single facility that is normally a central library.
>
> *Library.* The entire organizational entity and its units.
>
> *Manager.* This term is used generically to refer to the staff member or staff members who are responsible for resource allocation in a particular area; in some libraries, the "manager" is actually a team of staff members.
>
> *Team.* A group of staff members brought together to work on a specific project or program; often includes members from different departments and with different job classifications.
>
> *Unit.* A term used to refer to individual library departments and branches, if any.

Other Definitions

Each of the chapters in this book begins with a list of "New Vocabulary in This Chapter." All of the terms are defined in context during the course of the chapter. Many of these terms are also defined in the glossary at the end of the book.

Case Studies, Examples, and Workforms

Demonstrating Results follows two case studies through its chapters to help you see how the process of developing and implementing an outcome measurement plan might work in a "real" library. The library in both case studies is the Anytown Public Library, a mythical library somewhere in the United States that appears in most of the Results Series publications. The Anytown Public Library has an administrative board and serves a countywide population of 100,000 from a single building and a bookmobile. The case studies describe the development of outcome measurement plans for an Internet class for seniors and for a teen mother tutoring program. This book also includes a number of stand-alone examples to help explain certain concepts and ideas. Finally, the book includes fourteen workforms to help you collect and organize information. All of the workforms in this book are also available in electronic format from E-Learn Libraries (http://www.elearnlibraries.com).

Notes

1. Public Library Association Mission Statement, http://www.pla.org/factsheet.html.
2. Sandra Nelson, *The New Planning for Results: A Streamlined Approach* (Chicago: American Library Association, 2001).
3. Sandra Nelson, Ellen Altman, and Diane Mayo, *Managing for Results: Effective Resource Allocation for Public Libraries* (Chicago: American Library Association, 2000).
4. Diane Mayo and Jeanne Goodrich, *Staffing for Results: A Guide to Working Smarter* (Chicago: American Library Association, 2002).
5. Sandra Nelson and June Garcia, *Creating Policies for Results: From Chaos to Clarity* (Chicago: American Library Association, 2003).
6. Diane Mayo, *Technology for Results: Developing Service-Based Plans* (Chicago: American Library Association, 2005).
7. Institute of Museum and Library Services, *Outcome Based Evaluation,* http://www.imls.gov/grants/current/crnt_obe.htm.

Chapter 1

The What, When, and Why of Outcome Measurement

MILESTONES

By the time you finish this chapter you will be able to

- explain how outcome measurement differs from other planning and evaluation models
- understand the common philosophy of outcome measurement and *The New Planning for Results*
- describe the value of using outcome measurement
- determine whether a specific library program is suitable for outcome measurement

NEW VOCABULARY IN THIS CHAPTER

outcome	output
outcome measurement	objective
input	outcome statement

We all have wonderful anecdotes about the effects of library services on patrons' lives, warm and fuzzy human-interest stories that we (and our stakeholders) love to hear. You know what I mean: a regular user stops at the desk to tell us that he got a new job as a result of our resume-writing workshop. Or a mother reports that her children are doing better in school now that she can help them with their homework as a result of our literacy program. We share these tales with one another because they reflect the "So what?" of our services. Such successes are often used in media stories about the public library, or in the annual report, because they humanize our work. Rather than focus on what the library provides, these anecdotes show what happens to people *because* of what the library provides.

Outcomes are benefits to the end user that demonstrate the effectiveness of a program or service. Most of these benefits are changes in knowledge, skills, attitude, behavior, or condition. Note that these are accomplishments that the participant may or may not have experienced without the library program, but to which the library is a significant contributor. Outcomes can also be considered the key results or consequences sought by a user. Given these definitions of *outcome*, outcome measurement answers the question: *"What difference did our program make to the participant?"*

The impact, or outcome, of our program can be seen in gains for the user. Let's look at just one example of each of the major kinds of change or benefit. Note that they represent varied positions on a continuum from easy to difficult, or short-term to long-term outcomes. (See more on this in chapter 2.)

Knowledge. A job seeker has not found employment in her usual job category since her last employer moved operations out of state. As a result of a program in the library's job and career information center, she becomes aware that her job experience is transferable to three other job categories that she can pursue. She knows something new.

Skills. A novice in genealogy wants to research family history. As a result of a class in the library's genealogy center, he becomes adept at using the library resources for his research. He has a new skill.

Attitude. A father attends a parenting class at the library to learn about activities for his kindergartner. During the class he also hears about language-based activities for his newborn child. Although he had never thought of reading to a baby, he comes to realize that doing so might be beneficial for the infant. He changes his attitude or perception about emergent literacy. As a result of this change in perception, he resolves to begin reading to his baby. He has a new attitude and an intention to change a behavior.

Behavior. A junior high school student is failing math, in part because she never completes the assignments. She joins an after-school homework assistance program at the library, and finds that with a tutor she can understand the math problems that were too difficult for her before. Her skills improve. She begins completing and submitting her homework, and even speaks up in class. Her behavior has changed.

Condition or *status.* An immigrant uses the library to improve and practice her English language skills and to learn about the requirements for U.S. citizenship. She borrows an exam preparation book as well as language tapes. As a result of these library services, as well as other influences in her life, she passes the naturalization test and becomes a citizen. She has changed her status from green-card holder to citizen.

What Is Outcome Measurement?

Outcome measurement focuses on the quality and effectiveness of a program, and also allows us to quantify our users' success stories. Rather than report on one user who finds a job, or one adult new reader who can help her children, outcome measurement provides us with statistics so that we can report that "85 percent of people who complete our resume-writing workshop report getting job interviews; half of these report finding a new job." Or perhaps "95 percent of the adult learners who have been active in our family literacy program for at least six months demonstrate that they meet one of their personal goals as family members."

Here's a simple definition of outcome measurement. *Outcome measurement is a user-centered approach to the planning and assessment of programs or services that are provided to address particular user needs and designed to achieve change for the user.* Outcome measurement—also known as outcome-based evaluation, outcome assessment, or results-based evaluation—is a method of planning for and measuring program impact. Although outcome measurement may be a new term for many of us, outcomes are familiar. They are the intersection of community needs, service goals, and library service responses (activities). See figure 1.

FIGURE 1
What Is an Outcome?

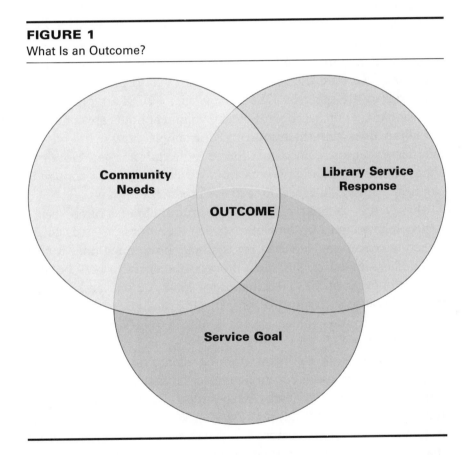

Don't Throw the Baby Out with the Bathwater

For-profit companies like to claim impacts on their customers. For example, Novartis—a cancer drug manufacturer—has been running an advertisement about a user who "is feeling so good he got married and recently had a baby boy." In other words, it is not enough to make claims for the drug's effectiveness in fighting cancer; Novartis tells us what wonderful things can happen to a person after its drug helps him to survive cancer. In addition, the advertisement exemplifies the fund-raising maxim that figures are important, but a human face and story are most compelling.

Many nonprofit agencies also stress their impacts. They use outcome measurement and report the results. For example, Kids Café—a free meal program of America's Second Harvest—reports that in 2003, "77 percent of parents/caregivers identified improvements in their child's learning since going to Kids' Café." Beyond fighting child hunger—its major goal—Kids' Café is having an impact on the children's education.

Naturally, America's Second Harvest still provides the customary statistics: how much food is donated, how much money is raised, how many tons of food are distributed, how many people eat how many meals. Similarly, libraries that use outcome measurement will still systematically measure their resources (inputs) and their activities and use (outputs). These statistics remain essential for both library management and stakeholders.

To use another example, a library will continue to track the cost of speakers (input) and the number of people who attend a lecture series (output) as well as the outcomes that may result from the series. A library will continue to record the price of postage (input) and the number of materials circulated in the books-by-mail program (output) even if it decides to measure the outcomes of that program.

Inputs and outputs are *library-oriented* statistics; they count what the library staff uses and does. *Inputs* are the resources libraries use to provide services. For example, how many dollars are spent on DVDs? How many FTEs are on the staff? How many large-print books are purchased? How many volunteer hours are contributed? *Outputs* are what the library does with the resources. For example, how many books did the library circulate? How many reference questions did the staff answer? How many programs did the staff present? Inputs and outputs are closely related; given enough resources (inputs), we can nearly always increase our activity products (outputs).

In addition to input and output measures, libraries often keep *process* measures that focus on how inputs become outputs. In other words, they calculate the relationship between resources and services. For example, how much does it cost—in both staff time and dollars—to select, purchase, process, and shelve a new book? What does it cost to provide books-by-mail to isolated users? Input, output, and process measures are all important because such information helps libraries assess their *efficiency*. The library's perceived value to stakeholders is usually related to these measures of the quality and quantity of *effort*.[1]

Of course, there are many other excellent ways to assess a library's value. For example, we can measure economic impact on the larger community, such as the value of attracting customers to nearby retail outlets. Or we can evaluate the cost-benefit or the return on investment (ROI) per taxpayer. We can monitor how well the library is doing in terms of utilization, customer satisfaction, or service quality. Keep in mind, though, that even if users are surveyed or interviewed in the process, these measures are still about the library. When we ask customers to rate their satisfaction with the library, we are asking about us, not about them. Some evaluators refer to this focus as "organization-referenced" results rather than the "person-referenced outcomes" that this book is about.[2]

In outcome measurement, the usual flow of inputs to outputs to goal is extended and broadened. Once the library has determined the outcomes, it uses inputs (resources such as staff, funding, facilities, expertise, collections, etc.) to create services and programs. The resulting outputs (products) lead to short-term user benefits (interim outcomes) that then lead to the achievement of other, longer-term user benefits (long-range outcomes). (See figure 2.)

FIGURE 2
Outcome Measurement Flowchart

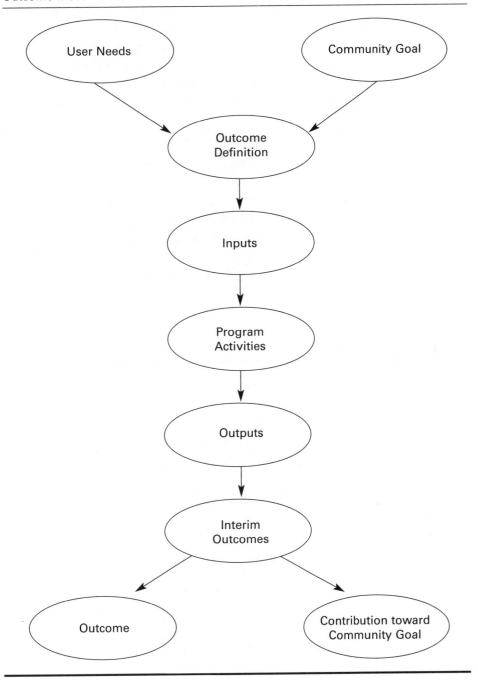

How does this work with *The New Planning for Results*? Libraries that use the *New Planning for Results* process can incorporate outcome measurement as part of monitoring their progress toward goals. The outcomes are identified after the library has selected service responses and written goals based on them, as illustrated in figure 3. Objectives are written for both outputs and outcomes. Libraries that have not used the *New Planning for Results* model—and have not selected service priorities—will identify outcomes as they are designing programs to meet a community goal. To see how *The New Planning for Results* and outcome measurement processes mesh, see figure 4.

Outcome Measurement Perspectives

The underlying premise of outcome measurement is that it is user-oriented, rather than library-oriented. As an aptly named journal article put it, "From the user in the life of the library, to the library in the life of the user."[3] Outcome measurement is about the user; its questions are *user-oriented*. For example, what has changed for the users as a result of our programs or services? How did our program make a difference in the lives of our users? By tracking the impact of their services and programs, libraries evaluate their *effectiveness*. We can then see the quality and quantity of *effect*. These results—or outcomes—are usually changes in knowledge, skill, attitude, behavior, or condition of the end user.

FIGURE 3
The New Planning for Results Flowchart

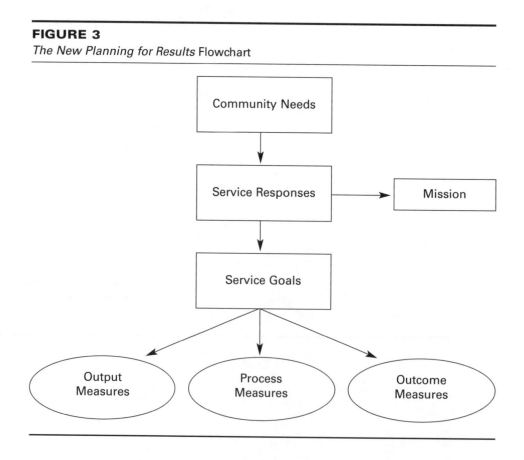

FIGURE 4
How *The New Planning for Results* and Outcome Measurement Work Together

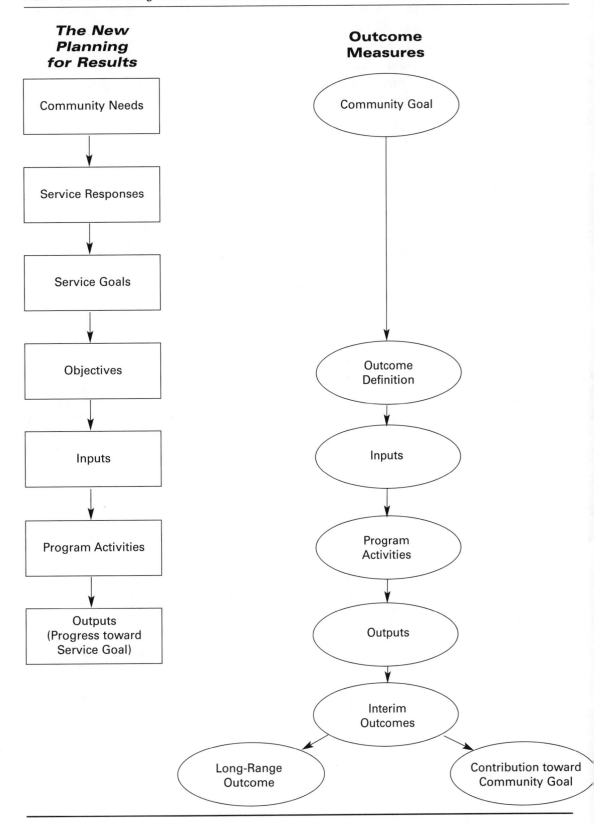

Outcome measurement stresses results rather than processes. Inputs, activities, and outputs are all staff-oriented because they tell what the staff has done. They are also pieces of the process of developing and evaluating programs and services. Interim outcomes, outcomes, and goals—in the outcome measurement approach—are all user-oriented and report on the results of our programs and services. (See figure 5.)

Traditionally, changes to library services have been made by directors, managers, and (sometimes) trustees who increase successful or popular programs and services, decrease underused or undervalued offerings, and try to maximize the library's resources. *The New Planning for Results* offers a better alternative to making decisions about services. It is a process that involves the community and then develops service responses based on community needs and goals, rather than the staff and board's perceptions of the library's needs or the current allocation of resources.

FIGURE 5
Outcome Measurement Perspectives

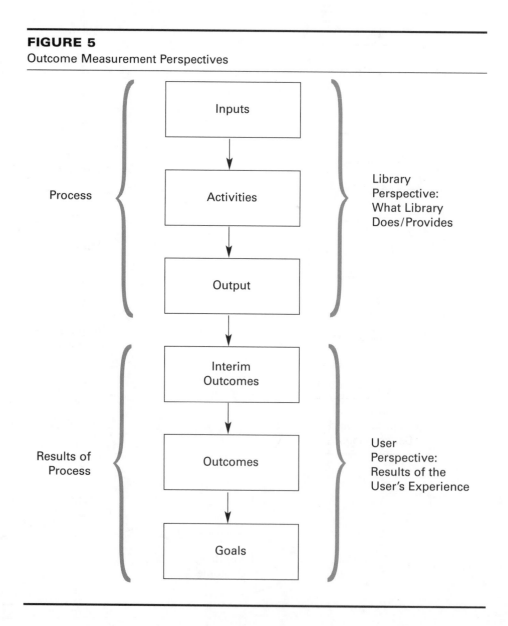

In the *New Planning for Results* process, goals are developed out of the community needs assessment and are statements of the ideal results of the library's selected service responses. Perhaps the most revolutionary aspect of this is that the goals are written with a focus on what the community (or specific members of the community) will receive, rather than what the library will do. Instead of "The Anytown Public Library will provide educational materials for school-age children," the goal might be, "Students in Anytown will have the resources they need to succeed in school."

In *The New Planning for Results*, objectives are statements of the way the library will measure its progress toward a goal. Libraries write one or more of three types of measures: number of users, how well the service meets the needs, and total units of service. Then an objective is written incorporating

- a measure (stated as a number), usually of library performance
- a standard of program success against which to compare that measure
- a time frame for completion

To continue the foregoing example, one *New Planning for Results* objective might be:

Measure: Percentage of middle school students in Anytown who use public library resources for homework help

Standard: 40 percent of the middle school children

Time frame: During the FY20— school year

The final objective: "During the FY20— school year, 40 percent of middle school students in Anytown will use public library resources for homework help." This is a prediction of participation (an output). Another objective, also a prediction of participation, might be: "The number of students who use the library homework help website will increase by 10 percent during FY20—."

When using outcome measurement, the library also writes objectives for its planned outputs. In addition, the library writes objectives (also known as outcome statements) for its anticipated outcomes. These objectives incorporate

- an outcome's indicators (a measurable behavior of a user)
- a quantity of that behavior (a standard of success for the user)
- a standard of program success
- a time frame for completion

To continue the example, a long-range outcome might be: "Middle school children who use the public library's resources for homework help will succeed in school."

Outcome indicator: Middle school children that use the public library resources for homework help will increase their grade

Quantity: In at least one subject by at least one grade

Standard of program success: 95 percent of the participants

Time frame: At the end of the semester

The final outcome measure statement (outcome objective): "95 percent of middle school children who use the public library's resources for homework help will increase their grade in at least one subject by at least one grade by the end of the semester."

SENIOR INTERNET CLASSES

Part 1

Objectives

In its biennial needs assessment, the Anytown Public Library found that older adults in Anytown ex-emplified the gap in Internet use that national studies had reported: people over age sixty-five were far less likely to access the Internet than people of other age groups. When asked how their quality of life could improve, many older adults stated that they would like to stay in closer touch with their grandchildren. Yolanda, head of user services, had read about the many libraries providing Internet classes specifically for seniors, and decided that Anytown should initiate this service too.

In writing up a proposal for the management team, Yolanda develops five objectives.

1. 2 one-hour classes per week will be held during January, February, and March. (This states the amount of what the library will do—an output.)

2. 25 older adults will participate in the three-month course. (This predicts the amount of attendance—an output.)

3. 75 percent of the participants will demonstrate their ability to use the mouse independently at the end of the first class. (This sets a standard for the percentage of participants who will demonstrate a change, who are now able to use the mouse independently—an outcome.)

4. 50 percent of the participants will independently participate in at least one e-mail correspondence after the first month. (This also predicts the percentage of participants who will demonstrate a change, who are now able to use e-mail—an outcome.)

5. 50 percent of the participants will report that they have developed and value a friendship with their tutors. (A long-range outcome representing a change for the user.)

Of those participants who master e-mail, 100 percent will report increased communication with their grandchildren at the end of the three-month course. (Again, a demonstration of a benefit for the user. In this case, it is a long-range outcome.)

Note two things about the case study. First, outcome measurement does not substitute for other measures. The library still tracked the number of classes offered and the number of attendees. Second, some outcomes occurred sooner than others; this will be discussed in more detail in the next chapter.

The Two Faces of Outcome Measurement

Planning and evaluation are always two sides of the same coin. In traditional planning, we decide the activities and services to provide; specify the inputs, outputs, and antici-pated use; and develop an action timeline. In most cases, success is defined as producing the specified amount of products or services, within the constraints of the inputs, by the end date. So a summer reading program is successful if the posters and other publicity materials are distributed, the anticipated number of children (or more) register, the story-tellers present their programs to standing-room-only attendance, and all the reading prizes are claimed by the end of August. In other words, evaluation is a confirmation that the planning and implementation were well done.

Outcome measurement, though, depends on knowing what happens as a result of a traditional success. To use the summer reading program example, all the outputs mentioned previously must occur. In addition, planners need to measure the changes that occur in children who have participated in the program. How do we know what those gains might be? In many of the case studies in the literature, *ongoing* programs have been examined for outcomes. Perhaps young readers are asked about their experiences and then parents and teachers are interviewed. Possibly researchers find that students who participate in the summer reading program return to school in the fall with a different attitude than students who have not been reading regularly. Perhaps the reading abilities of young participants improve during the course of the program. Whatever the researchers discover can be tested during the next summer's program. The difficulty is that libraries often develop *new* services or programs that they have not provided before, so they do not know what outcomes to look for. In the following chapter we will discuss how to predict outcomes. For the moment, it is enough to see that outcome measurement, even more than traditional forms of evaluation, is a planning tool as well as an evaluation technique. Sometimes the role of outcomes in planning is overlooked because outcomes are about ends rather than means.

One Size Does Not Fit All

The New Planning for Results states that excellence is achieved by meeting local needs, and that "one size fits all" is a fallacy. The same is true for outcome measurement; the outcomes and their indicators must be determined locally, in context.

Let's take an easy example: a literacy program. Most of us would agree that a successful library literacy program produces adult learners who can read better after they've experienced the program than they could before they enrolled. Indeed, traditional success can be defined as the ability to read at a higher level according to a standardized reading scale. But in outcome measurement, the question is always "So what?" If a person enrolls in the library literacy program to be able to pass an exam for promotion at work, passing the work exam is the real gauge of success. Another person may enroll to be able to read to his grandchildren; in that case, the ability to pass an exam is not in itself a definition of success. This concept is explored more fully in chapter 2.

Scientific or Pragmatic? Quantitative or Qualitative?

Many librarians express concern about their staff conducting "scientific research" or about needing to hire a research firm to do outcome measurement. But outcome measurement, as discussed in this book, is not scientific or experimental research. Although it has pieces that look like scientific research, our use of outcome measurement does not use the systematic methodology or standardized framework of social science. For example, we are not serving and assessing a carefully selected sample of people, and we do not have a control group for comparison purposes. We are not testing specific hypotheses or looking for information to generalize to other groups of people or other programs. Instead, we are looking for pragmatic information that we can use to meet needs and improve our programs. This type of study is often called "pragmatic" or "practical" research.

Besides allaying fears of outcome measurement, understanding this distinction will prove important when analyzing and using our results (as discussed in chapter 6).

Another common question about the research aspect of outcome measurement is whether it produces qualitative or quantitative information; these two types of data are traditionally distinct. *Quantitative* data is numeric and reports the quantity or frequency of something. Usually, the indicators of quantitative data are visible, easily measurable, and expressed in numbers. Circulation data and Internet terminal use data are examples of quantitative data commonly kept by public libraries. *Qualitative* data is experiential, reports on the quality or character of something from the user's perspective, and is expressed verbally. Customer satisfaction is an example.

But social scientists no longer see "quantitative" and "qualitative" as a polarized choice or even as mutually exclusive properties. Sometimes qualitative information can be handled in a quantitative fashion. Outcome measurement yields a hybrid of quantitative and qualitative data. One success story is qualitative, yet the fact that 50 percent of users have a similar success story can be expressed as quantitative data. Outcome measurement allows us to quantify anecdotes by collecting qualitative information that is analyzed as quantitative data. This will be discussed in more detail in chapters 4 and 5.

Why Use Outcome Measurement?

The easy answer to this question is that both the government and private funders are requiring outcome measurement. The U.S. Congress passed the Government Results and Performance Act (GRPA) in 1993, in response to growing calls for accountability by taxpayers. Other federal legislation, such as the Workforce Investment Act of 1998, requires outcomes as a demonstration of accountability and program quality. Outcome measurement has been in use, primarily in education and social services, since the 1980s. As a result of the GRPA, federal agencies—including AmeriCorps and the IMLS, which distributes LSTA funds to the states for grants to libraries—have adopted outcomes as required planning information for funding recipients. Many states and counties have developed parallel requirements for accountability reporting. Private funders, such as national and local foundations, have found that outcome measurement demonstrates the human face of what their funds provide, and that such demonstrations attract collaborators and donors to the causes they support. According to a 2003 study, 92.5 percent of national health and human services organizations now use outcome measurement.[4] These groups range from the American Cancer Society to Big Brothers/Big Sisters, the Girl and Boy Scouts, and the National Urban League. All four of the relevant national accrediting organizations require outcome measurement in their standards, too. The United Way, whose pioneering work formed the basis for much of what is being done now, has used outcomes since 1995. But besides funding requirements, here are eight other compelling reasons to measure outcomes.

1. *The New Planning for Results* stresses that libraries must base their activities on the needs of the community. Service responses are the library's acknowledgement of what the library can do to meet those needs. Outcome measurement is a process for the library to identify—and then measure—the indicators of achievement.

2. Outcome measurement forces us to make our assumptions explicit. Why do we think that providing bookmobile service will build a sense of community in a rural area? Why do we assume that preteens who read for pleasure are more likely to graduate from high school? Discussions about the community and about the library's role are stimulated (and stimulating). Also, staff enthusiasm for a favorite program often leads us to believe that it is working; we assume that it is because of staff desires and perceptions. Once we state what we expect to do, outcome measurement provides the empirical evidence that what was intended was achieved.

3. Outcome measurement is good for community collaboration. In order to design effective programs and services for outcome measurement, other agencies and individuals should be involved. This positions the library as a team player in the community. Meeting the needs of the users then demonstrates the library's contribution toward solving community problems.

4. Because measuring outcomes requires selecting interim outcomes as well as long-range outcomes, significant milestones are identified. Using the milestones keeps the implementation of a program or service on track. A milestone that is not reached forces staff to question the service delivery and to make midcourse changes in the "how" of a service, keeping an eye on the "why."

5. Outcome measurement focuses staff and stakeholders on the goals of a program or service by asking "So what?" at every turn. Teens are checking out more books. So what? What difference does it make to the young adults if they do or do not check out more books? What does it indicate about our aims? What the library does is not the point in itself; what the library does should bring users closer to *their* goals.

6. Program improvement and innovation can result when programs are assessed with outcome measurement. If expected outcomes are not reached, staff must consider whether the outcome is off-target or the library program must be revised to reach the outcome. If outcomes are achieved, staff may consider using parts of the program strategy in other library services.

7. Outcome measurement provides new insights into why and how library services are used, and allows staff (and volunteers) a new perspective. Most staff will be energized by the evidence that their work matters and makes a difference in people's lives. This emphasis on human impact gives all staff—in all units of the library and at all levels of the organizational chart—a common purpose and a new way to answer the question, "Why does the library do such and such?"

8. Outcome measurement is good for the library, too. It is a vehicle to determine the contributions that the library makes to the lives of its users. Once we know what those contributions are, we can use them as the basis of library publicity and fund-raising.

The benefits of using outcome measurement are impressive. But before we discuss this topic any further, we must also consider three caveats.

Cautions

1. Your library cannot assume all the credit (or all the blame) for any outcome or result. This is because our users participate in and benefit from many other services and influences. For example, family and employment issues, changes in other programs and services

the participants use, economic trends, and even natural disasters can influence the type and level of outcome achieved. The library can say that it is a contributor to change, but not the sole cause. The library can claim to be making a difference to people, and can know that its program is moving in the right direction.

2. Outcome measurement can tell us whether our program had the results we expected, but it cannot tell us why it did or did not. The use of interim outcomes and analysis by cross-tabulation, though, provide valuable clues.

3. Because outcomes are designed locally, based on context, outcome measurement usually does not give us results that can be generally applied to others. That is, we cannot use our results to compare our program with others. In some cases, outcomes may be broad enough to apply to many libraries (e.g., increased self-esteem, or advancement at work), but the indicators will be different depending on context. (For more about this, see chapter 3.)

Using Outcome Measurement in Your Library

Demonstrating Results provides a clear and easily understood process to help you and your colleagues use outcome measurement in your library. The tasks and steps in the process are listed in figure 6.

FIGURE 6
Overview of the Process

Task 1: Select a Program for Outcome Measurement

Task 2: Determine the Interim and Long-Range Outcomes

Step 2.1 Define candidate outcomes

Step 2.2 Test the candidate outcomes

Step 2.3 Select the outcomes to use

Step 2.4 Confirm the time frames for your outcomes

Task 3: Make Outcomes Measurable

Step 3.1 Specify indicators for each outcome

Step 3.2 Set a target for each indicator

Step 3.3 Compose outcome statements

Task 4: Design the Data Plan

Step 4.1 Review data collection methods

Step 4.2 Select a data collection method

Step 4.3 Create or adapt a data collection instrument

Step 4.4 Decide on data analysis needed

Step 4.5 Devise a data plan

Task 5: Prepare for Implementation

Step 5.1 Write an outcome measurement plan

Step 5.2 Address staff concerns

Step 5.3 Recruit and train data collectors

Step 5.4 Pilot-test the data plan

Step 5.5 Design an action plan

Task 6: Make the Most of Your Results

Step 6.1 Interpret your results

Step 6.2 Communicate your results

Step 6.3 Use your results to move forward

TASK 1: SELECT A PROGRAM FOR OUTCOME MEASUREMENT

Outcome measurement is appropriate for only some library services and programs in certain situations. Selecting a program or service suitable for outcome measurement is the first task in this process. You are strongly encouraged to select a program or service that is currently offered in your library—or that you plan to offer—to be used as a test case in order to help you understand the tasks and steps of outcome measurement. As you read the rest of this book, you will use the program that you identify in this task to understand the other six tasks in the process.

The most important criterion of suitability for outcome measurement is this: the program must be planned to meet the identified needs of a clearly defined group of end users. By *end users* we mean library customers or patrons, not staff or other internal customers. A second requirement is that the program should concentrate on results—impact on human beings—rather than process or product. A third criterion is that the program have a distinct beginning and end, or that the user's involvement in the service or program be limited so that it is possible to track the user's progress throughout the program. A corollary to this third criterion is that participation in the program requires more than one interaction with the library. The fourth criterion is that the program have clearly identifiable users. In other words, the library must be able to identify the users—though not necessarily by name—so that it can follow up on the program. Library programs directed at the whole community—such as a general publicity campaign—are not as well-suited to outcome measurement as programs for a specific, well-defined group of users.

Note that I keep using the term *program*. It is essential to differentiate between "programs," which are a set of related activities with a common purpose provided to a specific group of users with a common need; and a "service," which is defined as an ongoing series of programs and activities provided to all users. Programs, unlike services, usually have a distinct beginning and end, marked by either a time frame or a goal. Many services are user-oriented and results-focused, and so are theoretically suitable for outcome measurement. But it is usually much more difficult to evaluate an ongoing service than a time-limited program. In order to use outcome measurement on an ongoing service such as readers' advisory, it is necessary to create an arbitrary time frame. Similarly, it is more difficult to assess a one-time use of a service than a continued program interaction. In order to use outcome measurement on a one-time service such as reference, it is necessary to ask users about their intention at the time of the reference interaction, and to follow up only with users who have given their permission at that same time. (See more on this in chapter 4.)

Experience using outcome measurement shows that the programs best suited to outcome measurement share other criteria, too. These are:

- clearly defined mission
- stable program staff (including volunteers)
- supportive stakeholders, including the library administration
- a minimum of two years to plan, initiate a new program, and evaluate it

In most cases, technical services, administration, human resources, facilities management, purchasing, and other behind-the-scenes functions are not suitable for outcome measurement. For example, a change in the library's delivery system should increase the library's efficiency. But it should also be invisible to library users and affect them only indirectly. Therefore it is not suitable for outcome measurement. Other examples of projects that usually do not fit the criteria for outcome measurement are retrospective conversion, website design, and building construction.

Some services may impact end users by increasing access, but it will be difficult to measure such outcomes, at least in the near future. Examples include the Public Library Geographic Database, which gives demographic and location information to help public libraries plan; radio frequency identification systems that facilitate customer self-service; integrated library systems which allow patrons to interact with the library's circulation functions; and digitization projects that will make rare and fragile materials easily accessible to patrons.

A lecture series on public policy issues, however, should have a direct impact on participants' knowledge, attitudes, and behavior, and so is appropriate for outcome measurement. The same is true for information literacy programs and bilingual story hours. Homework help, preschool programs, outreach services, and literacy programs are all good candidates for outcome measurement. So-called high touch programs are, by their very nature, well-suited for outcome measurement. Readers' advisory services or reference services can fit this category too, if a time frame is imposed.

EXAMPLE 1

Public Programs on Death and Dying

The Anytown Hospital invited the Anytown Public Library to join with them in sponsoring a series of public television programs on death and dying, based on a recent Bill Moyers show on PBS. The intent of the TV programs was to encourage adults to take control over their own dying by opening discussion of end-of-life options and making personal decisions while they are still healthy. Because the program's stated intention was for people to take action of some sort, the series was clearly outcome-oriented. The hospital and library would count inputs (e.g., staff time spent, cost of producing publicity materials) and outputs (e.g., number of programs held, number of participants, number of newspaper articles generated) but would focus on outcomes. By speaking with other libraries and hospitals that had sponsored such programs, as well as people involved in the original Moyers production, they identified possible outcomes. These included changes in knowledge (e.g., of available options), changes in attitude (e.g., toward hospices), political actions (e.g., support of legislation for or against euthanasia), personal actions (e.g., purchase of long-term care insurance), and interpersonal actions (e.g., discussion with family members).

To decide whether or not the library program you are considering is suited to outcome measurement, discuss the following questions with your staff and colleagues:

Has this program or service been developed in response to an identified need?

Is impact on the end user a declared intention?

Does the program (or the user's involvement with it) have a distinct beginning and end?

Is the program more concerned with human benefit than with library outputs (products)?

Is it focused on public service rather than internal library operations?

Is it more concerned with effectiveness than efficiency?

If you can answer "yes" to those six questions, ask yourself:

Is the program stable enough to undertake such an endeavor? Programs that have a revolving door for staff or which depend primarily on volunteers may not be suitable for outcome measurement which takes concerted staff time.

Do the users participate consistently so you can track their progress?

Is the library leadership committed to dedicating resources to evaluation? Assessing even one outcome of a program will take time, money, personnel, and expertise.

Is the library leadership committed to acting on the results? Any kind of evaluation is an exercise in frustration if the administration is not interested in the results. Outcome evaluations show us how our programs and services affect people; if that information is not used to improve programs and to promote the library as a community collaborator and problem-solver, it may not be worth the time and effort to collect it.

Do the program management and staff have a service orientation? If not, they might not care whether the program produces outcomes for users.

Are the stakeholders involved and supportive? If not, can the results of the outcome evaluation change their perspective?

If the answers are still positive, use Workform 1, Program Suitability for Outcome Measurement, to continue the discussion about the suitability of the program among your staff and try to decide whether outcome measurement is appropriate for your program. When you have selected the program you want to use throughout the remainder of this book, you are ready to move on to chapter 2.

Key Points

Outcome measurement answers the question, "What difference did this program make to the user?"

Both outcome measurement and *The New Planning for Results* depend on understanding the needs of the local community.

Outcome measurement shifts the focus from what the library does to what impact the library has on users.

Outcome measurement focuses on effectiveness.

Outcome measurement is not appropriate for all library programs and services.

Libraries need to collect input, output, and other statistics even if they use outcome measurement.

Notes

1. This concept of quantity or quality of effort is from the Foundation Consortium for California's Children and Youth, http://www.foundationconsortium.org/site/commapp/rba/index.html.
2. Robert L. Schalock, *Outcome-Based Evaluation*, 2nd ed. (New York: Kluwer/Plenum, 2001).
3. M. Kyrillidou, "From Input and Output Measures to Quality and Outcome Measures, or From the User in the Life of the Library to the Library in the Life of the User," *Journal of Academic Librarianship* 28 (2002): 42–46.
4. United Way, *Outcome Measurement Activities of National Health and Human Service and Accrediting Agencies* (Alexandria, VA: United Way of America, 2003). The four national accrediting agencies surveyed are CARF (the Rehabilitation Accreditation Commission), the Council on Accreditation, the Joint Commission on Accreditation of Healthcare Organizations, and the Council on Quality and Leadership. Together they have accredited 22,675 national organizations, all of which use outcome measurement at the national or the community level.

Chapter 2

Determine Outcomes

MILESTONES

By the time you finish this chapter you will be able to

- give examples of interim and long-range outcomes
- explain why customer satisfaction and staff training are always interim outcomes
- determine the right long-range and interim outcomes to measure for your program by completing the five tasks presented here

NEW VOCABULARY IN THIS CHAPTER

interim outcomes	satisfaction outcomes
long-range outcomes	staff training outcomes
candidate outcomes	

Imagine that you happen upon three library staff members drinking coffee in the staff room and talking about their weekend. Azar says, "I had a scare yesterday. I'd been doing a lot of driving and had used a lot of gas, but I thought I had enough to get to the kids' school. But no, I ran out of gas and had to walk two miles in the rain to a gas station while the kids waited for me. I've made a resolution to never let the gas gauge fall below half again!" Mary says, "It sure was raining hard! I thought they'd cancel the dog obedience class, but they didn't. The teacher's really good. I'm not sure Chip is learning anything, but I sure am. I can get him to sit on command now." Chang shares his weekend story. "I went to the movies with a bunch of friends, and we were all amazed by that new documentary. We talked and talked about it afterwards. It really gave me a new perspective on the political process and may change my vote in the upcoming election."

All three staff members reported on consequences, or outcomes, of their weekend activities. Azar has changed her attitude toward her gas tank, and has vowed to change her behavior by filling up more frequently. Mary is behaving differently with her dog—something she learned in class—and can see the result when her dog sits. Chang learned something from the movie, participated in a discussion on the movie's content, and may change his voting behavior. In the staff room, people may call these the "results" of their activities or the "impact" of their experiences, but in outcome measurement, they are outcomes.

There is one major difference between Azar's outcomes and those of Mary and Chang, however. Azar's gas station adventure was the result of chance; she certainly had not planned to run out of gas. Mary and Chang, by contrast, received the benefits that were planned for their experiences. The obedience trainer has assumed that her human students would learn new skills; she has planned her lessons so that they can practice those skills; and they attend the class with the expectation that they will be able to get their dogs to obey. The film writer and director made a deliberately provocative movie, hoping it would affect viewers and inspire discussion and action.

In outcome measurement, the library plans programs that will result in outcomes for the users. Based on what users need, programs and services are designed to meet the need and have an impact—this is the planning side of outcome measurement. During and after the program, the library assesses whether or not the outcomes have been met—this is the evaluation side of outcome measurement.

EXAMPLE 2

Health Lecture Series

The Anytown Public Library has a new adult services manager, Aisha. She wants to offer library programs for seniors at the local nutrition center, so she does a simple needs assessment. She asks the older adults who gather there daily for lunches to select from a list of possible lecture topics. One of these, health, is by far the most popular. Aisha then develops a lecture series on the prevention and cure of six common diseases that older adults typically face; a guest lecturer speaks after lunch on one of the diseases every Wednesday over a six-week span. Aisha notices that even though the evaluations for each speaker are excellent, very few participants stay for more than one of the lectures. In one-to-one conversations with the seniors, she asks whether she had picked the wrong diseases, or whether people only attended the lecture about the one disease most relevant to their lives. She found out that neither of these was the reason for the intermittent attendance. She discovered that people were interested primarily in medications, rather than prevention and cure. When people had completed the needs assessment survey, they had thought that they would learn about alternative medications that they might want to ask their doctors about and how to take their medications more effectively. If Aisha had asked people about the outcomes they hoped to achieve, she would have developed a very different program series.

Interim and Long-Range Outcomes

At this point it is necessary to differentiate between interim and long-range outcomes. *Interim outcomes,* also called *initial* or *intermediate* outcomes, are the initial results for the patron. These benefits or changes are the first in a sequence of events that will lead to a long-range outcome. Interim outcomes usually are visible and measurable within a year of the beginning of a program, so they are often referred to as *initial* or *short-term outcomes.* But in some cases, it may take one to three years for the changes to be tangible; often these outcomes are called *intermediate outcomes.* All interim outcomes answer the question: "What is the *short-term benefit* to the user from this library program?"

Long-range outcomes are benefits for the user that do not become visible and measurable until a minimum of two years after the beginning of the program. They are fundamental, complex, and meaningful achievements. Depending on the situation, library users may need to participate in the designated program for two to five years. Sometimes long-term participation in the library program is not necessary, but a time lapse of two to five years may be needed to achieve the outcome. Long-range outcomes answer the question: "What difference did our program make to the user in the long run?"

For example, your library, based on community needs, may decide to offer workshops in the use of electronic information so that people can use it competently and independently. An initial outcome might be that the participants can differentiate among three types of electronic resources. This is a change in users' knowledge or skill level, but it is only a necessary step en route to the patrons' long-range outcome. A second interim outcome may be that the participants can find reliable, objective, accurate, and current information in different electronic resources. This, too, is a change in the users' knowledge or skill level. Again it is a step on the way to a long-range outcome. The long-range outcome might be that participants meet a personal or educational goal using information that they found in electronic resources. In other words, the impact that the library workshop has on participants is that it enables them to meet their own educational or personal goals. Remember that a long-range outcome is a key result sought by the user.

Think about another example. Your library decides, based on community needs, to offer preschool story hours coupled with parenting classes to help increase school readiness among children entering elementary school (the community goal). An immediate outcome might be that parents enroll in the parenting classes and attend regularly. Assuming that they were not in parenting classes previously, this is a change in their behavior. Ditto with attending preschool story hours. But these are only steps on the way to the more significant, long-range outcome that parents nurture early literacy development in their homes and in their children's lives.

Note that an interim outcome may be identical to an output; in this situation the output is considered a proxy outcome. In the preceding example, attendance at a parenting class is usually considered an output, a usage statistic. But since the library cannot teach the parents how to nurture early literacy in their children unless the parents attend the class, attendance becomes an essential step en route to the outcome. So interim outcomes answer this question too: "What will the user do that is necessary if he or she is to achieve the long-range outcome later?"

Interim outcomes play a significant role for the library as well as for the user. They are milestones in the life of a project, events that are necessary for successful long-range outcomes. As milestones, they are critical points at which staff must decide whether to continue current activities or modify them in order to achieve the desired long-range outcomes. Continuing with the example, if no parents register for the parenting classes, something is wrong with the program design or publicity, and the library must change course. Since outcome measurement is focused on the ends and not the means, making adjustments is considered a positive move on the part of the library. For a library that is only collecting outputs, the fact that 200 posters had been designed, printed, and distributed looks good. But in outcome measurement, the posters are considered a means to an interim outcome, a way to attract parents to the classes. If parents don't come, the value of the posters must be reconsidered.

Another common interim outcome is user satisfaction, because it is necessary for users to be satisfied with a service in order for them to use it repeatedly. If the users do not use the program frequently, the long-range outcomes of the program cannot be achieved. Again, the library may need to make changes in its customer service policies or procedures to ensure the success of the program.

TASK 2: DETERMINE THE INTERIM AND LONG-RANGE OUTCOMES

Step 2.1
Define Candidate Outcomes

The first step in determining outcomes is to talk with people about how your program might benefit users. The easiest place to start is with members of your own staff who serve your intended participants. Brainstorm by asking, "Which users will *benefit* from this service or program, and how?" Then ask, "In the best of circumstances, what other *benefits* might there be for those participants?" Ask: "What difference does this program make to the users?" and "How do we define success for the participants (not for the library, but for the participants)?"

It may help to discuss the possibility of each type of benefit, one by one. What change in *knowledge* might result from this program? What *skills* would be different as a result of our program? What change in *attitude or perception* might result? How might the user's *behavior* be different? What change in *condition or status* might result?

Talking with staff will yield a partial list of *candidate outcomes*. A candidate outcome is a potential or proposed outcome that has yet to be reality-checked. It is based on the staff members' knowledge and assumptions about the participants. You will hear, and record, candidate interim and long-range outcomes during your discussion with library staff.

Program records and logs can provide another source of information about candidate outcomes. You may find that outcomes have been noted informally. Ask staff and others for anecdotes and testimonials they have heard. Again, these are candidate outcomes because they still need to be verified by users and others. Note that staff members may be surprised or even offended that you will check these outcomes with users, because they are confident that they know what library users need. One of the side benefits of using outcome measurement is that it forces us to reconsider our assumptions.

Next, talk with staff and volunteers who work directly with your intended participants elsewhere in the community. Ask: "What difference would this program make to participants?" "What changes might we see in participants if our program is successful?" and "What other benefits might there be for the participants?" You will undoubtedly uncover candidate interim and long-range outcomes. Follow up by asking, "How will we know that the outcome has been achieved? What will we see that demonstrates the change?" This second set of questions will elicit candidate indicators. (See chapter 3 for more on indicators.)

If your program is ongoing, or if you have had a similar program in the past, it is critical that you interview or hold focus groups with current and past participants. Ask current users: "If this program really helps you, how will you be better off?" or "What do you expect to change for you as a result of this program?" Ask users in a prior program: "What has happened to you as a result of that program?" or "How is your life different now because of that program?" This is the moment to test your candidate outcomes by asking both current and past participants, "Is it reasonable to think that such and such might result from this program?" Again, ask, "How will we know that the outcome has been achieved?" "What will we see that demonstrates the accomplishment?"

Finally, you should talk with representatives of agencies that might be the "next step" for your intended participants. Ask: "What will participants need to know or be able to do in order to succeed in your program?" "What do you see as the value in our program preceding yours?" By the time you have finished this step, you should have a list of candidate outcomes for your selected programs. (See Tool Kit A, Sample Candidate Outcomes, for sample candidate outcomes from library and other programs.)

Now draft a sentence for each of the candidate outcomes. When expressing an outcome, always keep in mind that outcomes are impacts on participants and usually are changes in their knowledge, skills, attitude, behavior, or condition. The outcome should be stated as, "The participant/user/child/adult will. . . ." Remember that the library is not mentioned in the program outcome.

An outcome is fairly broad and general. The specific behavior that will indicate that the outcome has been reached will be selected later, in Task 3. Therefore, most outcomes use general verbs that suggest a direction of change, such as "increase" or "decrease." See figure 7 for more outcome verbs.

Be cautious about using outcomes that are too broad; for example, "improved quality of life." Quality of life has many dimensions, including social inclusion and interpersonal relationships; physical, emotional, and spiritual well-being; and economic and employment status.

You should have written a statement with a subject (user), a verb, and an object (what will be changed) for each candidate outcome. Record those statements on Workform 2, If-Then Exercise.

Step 2.2
Test the Candidate Outcomes

The second step is to test the candidate outcomes to be sure that they are related logically to your program. An easy way to do this is to use the *if-then exercise*.[1] In this exercise, you write out statements of expectation and see if they are reasonable. The *if* side

FIGURE 7
Outcome Verbs

understand
attain
increase
improve
decrease
reduce
expand
enhance
alter
change
gain

expresses the program's practice, and the *then* side reflects an expected outcome. If the program does such and such, then we can assume such and such benefit to the participants. For example, if the proposed library program is homework assistance, and the community goal is greater rates of employment for young adults, think (or write) through these steps:

- *If* the library provides students with assistance with their homework → *then* the students will do better at their schoolwork. *If* they do better at school → *then* they will get better grades and attend school more regularly.

- *If* they get better grades and attend school more regularly → *then* they are more likely to graduate. *If* they graduate → *then* they are more likely to become employed.

Does this chain of causal assumptions make sense? In general, yes. But you need to reality-check it based on your discussions with other people in the preceding step. Do these interim outcomes seem reasonable? Are there other interim or long-range outcomes that were suggested that do not appear in the chain? Should they be added?

Let's take another example:

- *If* the library sends books-by-mail to isolated older adults → *then* the recipients will have something to read.

- *If* the recipients have something to read → *then* they will be less lonely.

Does this chain make sense? No, it does not. There is a gap between having reading materials and being less lonely. What needs to be revised so that the assumptions are reasonable? One possibility is that the program needs revision. For example, a book discussion program for books-by-mail recipients, facilitated by the library, and held by phone, would allow isolated older adults to talk with others and thereby be less lonely. Another possibility is that the outcome needs reconsideration. For example, if the recipients have something to read, then they will find that their days are more pleasurable.

Note that if you do not yet have a program in mind, but want to develop one for a given community goal, the "if-then" chain will work from intended results back to potential services. If your community goal is a higher employment rate among young adults, consider (write) the chain of expectations like this:

- *If* we want more young adults to be employed → *then* they must be prepared with a high school education. *If* we want more young adults to graduate from high school → *then* we need them to attend school more regularly and to get better grades.

- *If* we want them to do better in school → *then* we need to offer them assistance with their homework.

Use Workform 2 to develop if-then statements for the candidate outcomes you have identified.

Just as this is making sense to you, we must add one other aspect to the concept of outcomes. Any program may have impacts on more than one group of people. For example, preschoolers at story time are accompanied by their parents or caregivers. Are there outcomes you want to measure about the adults' experience of story time? Another example is that homework assistance may have outcomes for the volunteer providers as well as for the students.

By the time you have finished Step 2.2, you should have tested each candidate outcome to see if it can flow logically from your program. You have probably discarded some candidate outcomes but have a few left.

Step 2.3
Select the Outcomes to Use

The third step in determining program outcomes is to make a final selection among all the candidate outcomes you have listed on Workform 2 and, by using the if-then exercise, have determined are connected logically to your program. Select outcomes that are valuable for the participants, important to the library, achievable by the program, politically compelling, and sensitive. "Valuable" outcomes are ones based on the participants' needs and are related to significant gains for them. Using the Case Study of the "Senior Internet Classes," for example, if you could measure only one outcome, it should be a benefit for the seniors, not for the teens or the grandchildren. "Important" outcomes are ones closely related to the library's missions and priorities. "Compelling" means that the outcomes are easy to explain to stakeholders who will appreciate what you find out. "Sensitive" means the outcomes are both culturally and contextually sensitive (i.e., they are relevant to your actual participants in their specific environment).

On the practical side, the selected outcomes should be achievable so you don't set yourself up for failure on your first foray into outcome measurement. Finally, be sure that your outcomes are in areas that you would like to draw attention to or to improve. Use Workform 3, Outcome Selection, to evaluate your outcomes.

GUIDELINES FOR FIRST-TIME USERS

Assuming that this is the library's first attempt at outcome measurement, you will probably want to start with only one long-range and one interim outcome per program.

Another time, you may choose to select more outcomes for your program. During this, your first outcome measurement experience, as you track the outcomes you've selected, you will also note any unexpected outcomes. It could be that next time you will want to track a different outcome or an additional outcome that you become aware of during this cycle.

Keep in mind that it is impossible to measure all outcomes, or even to perfectly measure one specific outcome. This is not scientific research, but an attempt to uncover vital information on how your library makes a difference to users in order to help the library improve its services.

By the time you have finished with this step, you will have selected one (or more) outcomes that you will aim for and assess in your program.

Step 2.4
Confirm the Time Frames for Your Outcomes

The last step in this task is to double-check that the selected outcomes are correctly divided into interim and long-range outcomes. Outcomes range from immediate and fairly simple ones, such as awareness of a service, to long-range and fundamental ones, such as a change in social status. As you have seen in the last chapter, interim outcomes (sometimes called immediate or intermediate outcomes) occur sooner than long-range outcomes. That makes them easier for us to measure. Another way to look at the differences in outcomes is that changes or accomplishments that are more critical or significant for people are those that require more time and effort.

FIGURE 8
Outcomes Continuum

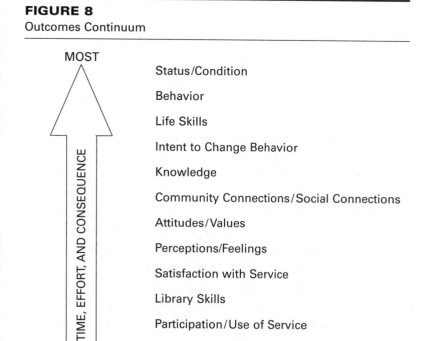

Source: Based on work in Michael Quinn Patton, *Utilization-Focused Evaluation* (Thousand Oaks, CA: Sage, 1997); and Jane Reisman and Judith Clogg, *Outcomes for Success!* (Seattle, WA: Evaluation Forum, 2000).

Figure 8 shows the continuum. Changes in individuals usually occur in approximately the order given, from bottom to top. The most difficult, complex, and time-consuming changes are those at the top of the continuum. These changes are intensive, are most significant in people's lives, and are therefore long-range outcomes. The changes at the bottom of the continuum are about the user's relationship to the library. These are the simplest, and can happen the fastest with the least effort by the user. For that reason, they are always immediate (or interim) outcomes. Note that a person does not necessarily go through all these changes in this or any other order. In other words, a person doesn't need to change their community connections in order to change their behavior. The continuum only shows that, for most people, changing community connections is an easier outcome to achieve than changing condition or status.

Condition or *status* outcomes include changing jobs, returning to school, or becoming a citizen. *Behavior* includes presenting oneself differently in job interviews, attending school regularly, or independently and successfully researching a topic of interest. Behavior can also mean progress toward a self-selected goal in areas such as health or literacy.

Skills and *knowledge* outcomes are the most familiar to us because of the library's role in lifelong learning. Knowledge refers to understanding an idea or comprehending a topic, while skills are applied knowledge or competence at a specific task. Learning a new idea or a new skill can be difficult and typically precedes a change in behavior.

Midway on the continuum are gains in *community connections* or *social networks*. This usually refers to users feeling more part of a community or less isolated, but it can also refer to political activity or recreational options.

Next are changes in *attitudes* or *values*. Social scientists debate whether attitudes precede behavior or vice versa. Say a person votes (a behavior) for the first time. Does this reflect a new attitude toward elections? Or does the act of voting cause the voter to alter her point of view on elections? For the sake of outcome measurement, we assume that changes in attitudes and values can—if not necessarily—occur before changes in behavior. The relationship between attitudes and behavior is a very complex issue; you don't need to be an expert on the subject as long as you're aware that attitudes and behaviors are mutually reliant.

One such attitude change is *intent to change behavior*, which is always an intermediate outcome since good intentions are never the same as a tangible accomplishment.

Changes in *perceptions* and *feelings* usually happen before changes in attitude. For example, sociologists have found that if people interact with someone from a different race or ethnic group and, from that interaction, change their perceptions of that person, they are very likely to change their attitudes and even their behavior toward other people in that racial or ethnic group. In terms of outcomes, perceptions and feelings include self-esteem and personal efficacy.

Awareness of service, *use* of service (including increased access), *satisfaction* with service (including savings of time and money), and *library skills* all appear in the lower section of the continuum and are all interim outcomes. They are easier and faster to achieve than other outcomes, and they share a significant characteristic—they are about the user's relationship to the library. Anything that is about the library is, by definition, an interim outcome. When we change people's perception and use of our services, we are helping ourselves as much as helping them. Of course, a program that increases users' satisfaction with the library (interim outcome) may have another interim outcome or a long-range outcome that is significant for the user. We must always ask: "What difference will it make to the user that he or she is more satisfied with the library services? Does this mean that he or she will use the library more regularly? What difference will that make to the user?"

Looking back at the outcomes continuum (figure 8), you can see that all of the categories above *library skills* can be intermediate or long-range outcomes, depending on your specific program and its users. Usually, the easiest way to differentiate between long-range and interim outcomes for any program is to set the long-range outcome first. Once you have determined that, all interim outcomes are below it on the continuum.

To ensure that your interim outcomes and long-range outcomes are appropriately labeled, try the "So what?" exercise in Workform 4, Interim and Long-Range Outcomes. Take an outcome and ask yourself and your staff "So what?" until you've reached an obvious long-range outcome. Using the previous example, I might say, "The patron is more satisfied with the library job and career information center than before." A staff chorus responds, "So what?"

"The patron will therefore use the library job and career information center more often."

"So what?"

"The patron will register for a public workshop such as resume writing."

"So what?"

"The patron will learn how to write a resume, will write and submit one to jobs listed in our database, and (perhaps) locate a job."

In this case, getting a job is the final *so what*, or long-range outcome (sometimes called an end outcome). The library might measure the initial outcome of satisfaction and another interim outcome: using the new resume to apply for a job. The final outcome of getting a job is dependent on too many factors—other than the quality of a resume—that the library cannot control.

EXAMPLE 3

College Test Preparation Course

The Anytown Public Library provides tutoring and after-school homework help for K–12 students and proctors for the SAT and other college admissions tests. Kim, one of the youth services librarians, proposes offering test preparation classes.

Modeled on those given by for-profit companies, the classes will teach test-taking skills with the community goal of increasing the number of students in the local high school that are accepted for college. The advertisements by the for-profit companies trumpet, "Make that dream come true. Go to college now!" but Kim realizes that whether the teens are actually admitted to college is beyond the control of the library, so she rewords the library's publicity to say, "Score higher on the SAT than you'd ever hoped!"

This is her long-range outcome for the program. The interim outcome is that the class participants will improve their scores on a sample SAT test at least 50 points from their PSAT scores by the end of the course.

Determining how short term our interim outcomes are, and how long range the others are, requires careful consideration. You must balance two truths. One is that the more immediate the outcome, the more influence your program has. The other is that time is needed to reach a meaningful outcome for the user. In other words, you want to select an outcome that is far enough in the future to allow for it to reflect the full benefits of the program without being so long range that the library's influence is no longer recognizable.

For example, a library job and career information center helps some users determine what jobs they are suited for, other users to locate appropriate job listings, and still others to write a resume. The personal goal for all the users is to find a new or better position.

Is the long-range outcome to find a job or to be prepared to find one? After all, whether or not a person finds a job is well beyond the power of the library; the economy and the individual's characteristics are most critical. Yet the information a person obtains and the skills she develops at the library may be a significant factor. A library can decide that the long-range outcome varies among users, depending on what sort of assistance they request.

Let's use literacy programs as another example of this decision point. People register for literacy programs because they want to learn to read. Each participant has specific reasons for wanting to read. Some want to qualify for a job or a promotion, some want to read to their children or grandchildren, and some want to be able to read a religious text such as the Bible. Reading children's books requires less skill than reading the Bible. The participants' stated personal goals can be used as the long-range outcomes; once the person meets the first personal goal, he or she can select a second personal goal to work toward. But what are the interim outcomes? Is participating in literacy activities, such as tutoring, sufficient? Is improvement of reading in general? The decision of where to set the interim and long-range outcomes is a difficult one. A solution is to use a somewhat generic and global long-range outcome, such as "Literacy participants will be able to read well enough to reach their personal goals." As we'll discuss in chapter 3, the specificity of the indicators allows for the long-range outcome to be broad.

CASE STUDY

SENIOR INTERNET CLASSES

Part 3

Outcomes Continued

Revisiting the Anytown Public Library's senior Internet classes, we see that two candidate outcomes are the same for both the seniors and their teen tutors. These are intergenerational understanding and new friendships. Probably new friendships should be a long-range outcome, because it takes a while to develop a friendship and to see if it has lasting value. The fact that other variables will intervene over time does not matter because the new relationship is based on e-mail use and therefore can continue.

Increased self-esteem, a candidate outcome for the teens, is a more difficult long-range outcome because a myriad of other situations and relationships—as well as increasing age and maturity—will affect self-esteem. It is difficult to determine what part of that change is due to the library.

By the time you have finished this step, you should have at least one interim outcome and one long-range outcome selected and described in simple sentences. At this point, return to Workform 4 and make any necessary revisions to the interim and long-range outcomes you have drafted there.

STAFF TRAINING OUTCOMES

We cannot leave the discussion of outcomes without considering one more specific type: *staff training outcomes*. Training is, by definition, an outcome-based activity since the goal is always impact on the trainees; the purpose is to stimulate or contribute to a change. Training users has at least one clear-cut outcome: to change their knowledge or skill level so that they can do something new or better. So it logically follows that the evaluation of user training should assess the impact on the learner (user).

When we train library staff, the situation is less clear. Our intent is to facilitate the staff in learning something new (change in knowledge), altering an attitude (change in attitude), or improving how they do something (change in skill or behavior). If we evaluate only how well the staff member learns, we are not considering the end user. Since benefit to the end user is the focus in outcome measurement, we need to look at how training staff can ultimately impact users. Because changes in staff knowledge, skills, attitude, and behavior may be prerequisites for an impact on the user, staff training is often considered an interim outcome. In order to keep user outcomes paramount, any planning and evaluation of staff training must ask both "What change does the library expect of the staff trainees?" and "What change do we expect the training to facilitate for users?"

Staff training varies in impact. Making the staff aware of a policy, for example, may have little result for the library user. Training staff to teach adult learners to read may contribute to a major change for the user. Note that the staff's reaction to or satisfaction with training is not a real outcome; it is a measure of the training itself rather than of the training's effect on the participants. There is more information on measuring the outcomes of staff training in Tool Kit B, Measuring Staff Training Outcomes.

EXAMPLE 4

Customer Service Training

The Anytown Public Library provides customer service training for all new employees. For many years, the evaluation has centered on the employees' opinions about the trainers, handout materials, schedule, and so on. This type of evaluation has been helpful to the administration; it has kept them apprised of what the employees expect and whether or not the trainers should be retained. Now that they are using outcome measurement in other areas, the library management team decides to try outcome measurement for the customer service training. They decide that the intermediate outcome is a change in skills and attitudes of the employees. One indicator is whether the staff member greets every customer in a welcoming manner; another is whether the staff member asks each customer if there is anything else he or she needs. The evidence will be clear to a trained observer. Higher customer satisfaction among library users will be the long-range outcome of the staff training. The library does a customer satisfaction survey every two years and will be able to use the satisfaction ratings to determine whether the training has been successful in terms of the long-range outcome.

Now complete Workform 5, Inputs, Outputs, and Outcomes, in which you describe your program's inputs, outputs, and outcomes. This is the foundation of your outcome measurement plan, which is sometimes called a "logic model" because it shows the causal links among needs, activities, inputs, outputs, and outcomes. (Refer back to figure 2 to see this relationship in flowchart form.)

Key Points

Interim outcomes are short-term benefits for the user.

Interim outcomes are also milestones in a program, opportunities for library staff to make changes.

Long-range outcomes express the "So what?" of the interim outcomes.

Long-range outcomes are more difficult for users to achieve, and are more fundamental to their lives.

Determining your program outcomes always requires talking to other people, inside and outside the library.

User satisfaction is always an interim outcome.

Staff training is always an interim outcome.

A new outcome measurement program should start by measuring only one outcome.

Note

1. The if-then exercise has been adapted from two books: Harry Hatry and others, *Measuring Program Outcomes: A Practical Approach* (Alexandria, VA: United Way of America, 1996); and Kristine L. Mika, *Program Outcome Evaluation: A Step-by-Step Handbook* (Milwaukee, WI: Families International, 1996).

Chapter 3

Make the Outcomes Measurable

MILESTONES

By the time you finish this chapter you will be able to

- explain the concept of context
- determine and test indicators of your selected outcome
- set targets for your program
- write a complete outcome statement
- respond to critics who want to misuse outcome measurement results

NEW VOCABULARY IN THIS CHAPTER

indicators   context

targets   outcome statement

standards of success

In the last chapter, you determined interim and long-range outcomes for your program. Now it is time to specify *indicators* of success for the individual participants in your program and *targets* of success for the overall program. When you have done this, you will be able to write outcome statements for your program. Outcome statements provide specific information about what you expect to happen to specified numbers of participants as a result of your program and the time frame in which you expect these results to happen. Outcome statements are the equivalent of objectives in *The New Planning for Results* and other planning processes. You can see this relationship in figure 4 in chapter 1.

TASK 3: MAKE OUTCOMES MEASURABLE

Step 3.1
Specify Indicators for Each Outcome

Outcome indicators—sometimes called change indicators—describe a specific change or action on the part of the user. By making the outcomes tangible, the indicators make the outcomes measurable. By the end of Step 3.1, you will have specified one or more indicators for each of your outcomes.

BEHAVIORS

Think of indicators as the operational definition of an outcome, or as evidence of an outcome. The evidence is displayed in a behavior. For example, an outcome may be that teens think independently. What does a teenager *do* that demonstrates independent thinking? We must specify the behavior or behaviors that substantiate the outcome of thinking independently.

Indicators are about the participants, not the program. Indicators answer the questions: "How will we know that the participants experienced the expected benefit or change?" "What will we observe, hear, or read that will tell us the outcome has been achieved?" "How can we gauge the outcome or the achievement for the participant?"

You will have asked other agencies and individuals about indicators when you were gathering candidate outcomes earlier in the process. But you may not have discovered all the possible indicators—or the indicators that are best for your program. Keep the suggested indicators in front of you as you read this chapter and decide which indicators to use.

Although indicators and outcomes are closely linked, it is essential to remember that they are not the same thing. An indicator is a tangible measure, an operational criterion, while an outcome is broader and more abstract. As noted in chapter 2, most outcomes use general verbs that suggest a direction of change, such as "increase" or "decrease." (See figure 7 for more outcome verbs.) Indicators, on the other hand, contain very specific measures of change that actually demonstrate an accomplishment. For example, in a job information program, an expected interim outcome might be that participants learn of new job and career options. One possible indicator would be that participants can list more appropriate jobs or career possibilities after the program than before. To show that they have experienced a change in knowledge (outcome), participants will list job options that they had not listed before. (How they will list them—in a test, a survey, or an interview—is the subject of chapter 4.)

QUANTITY OF BEHAVIOR: THE STANDARD FOR THE PARTICIPANT'S GAIN

An indicator can also be defined as a statistic that summarizes the user's achievement of an outcome, which raises the next question. What is our standard for participant success? What quantity of the indicator behavior do we expect the user to attain? Avoid terms like "substantial improvement" and "acceptable level" because they are too vague. Instead, use "a 25 percent increase," "double" the original number, or some other specific number.

In the job information center example, the program may specify that participants must be able to identify four more job options. Not just "four" but "four more." If the indicator specified just four job options, you would not know much about the amount of change—reaching a specific number may be a large or small gain. If the person started the program able to list three job options, listing four is a small change compared to the participant who knew of no options before the program.

INDICATOR CHARACTERISTICS

An indicator has a verb, an object for the verb, a quantity, and a time frame. The indicator verb is often obvious from the identified outcome. In a library orientation program, the verb and object are "find and use library resources," or more specifically, "use the OPAC." In a test preparation class, the verb and object are "pass the exam." In an introductory computer class, the verb and object might be "use the mouse"; in a more advanced class, it may be "access online databases."

In a literacy program, the verb is "read." What is read (the object) and how much is read (the quantity), however, must be decided upon. One criterion for making those decisions is whether the choices you make tell a story. A well-selected indicator and outcome pair describes a situation that makes the impact of the program clear. One such indicator might be that the participant reads an easy reader book with her grandson for the first time. Another might be that the participant reads the directions on the medication bottle without needing assistance. In both of these indicators, it is obvious that these are benefits or gains for the participant.

Another component of an indicator is a time frame. Time frames can be specified in three ways. You might specify a reporting period such as "during the next six months." Or you might specify an end date such as "by December 31, 2005." Or you might specify a length of time between two points such as "after the course as compared to before the course."

Let's look at the job information center example again to see some specific examples of outcomes and indicators.

> *Interim outcome:* Participants learn of new job or career opportunities
>
> *Indicator:* Participant lists four more job options after the program than before the program
>
> > Verb: *lists*
> >
> > Object of verb: *job options*
> >
> > Quantity: *four more*
> >
> > Time frame: *after the program than before the program*

The job and career information center may have specified, "can write a good resume by the end of the workshop" as another interim outcome. *Good* is an appropriate term for an interim outcome, but it is too vague to be a part of an indicator. The indicator will have to include a definition of the term *good*, as it does in this example.

> *Interim outcome:* Participants can write a good resume
>
> *Indicator:* Participant writes a resume that is rated as good or excellent by the workshop trainer by the end of the workshop

Verb: *writes*

Object of verb: *resume that is rated as good or excellent by the workshop trainer*

Quantity: *a* (one)

Time frame: *by the end of the workshop*

To carry this example to its logical conclusion, the long-range outcome of the program presented by the job information center is that participants get jobs. In this case, the outcome and the indicator are similar.

Long-range outcome: Participants will get a job

Indicator: Participant gets a job within one year of the program

Verb: *gets*

Object of verb: *job*

Quantity: *a* (one)

Time frame: *within one year of the program*

As you can see in each of these three examples, the indicator is specific and unambiguous. It can be measured or observed and it is time-bound. These indicators will provide clear evidence of the participant's success.

CASE STUDY

TEEN MOTHER TUTORING PROGRAM

Part 1

Indicators

The Anytown Public Library has a successful teen mother tutoring program. Graduation from high school is the long-range outcome, and the indicator is receipt of a diploma. An interim outcome is succeeding in school. This interim outcome has two indicators. The first is an improved attendance record, defined as having missed no more than one day per week during the past semester. The second indicator is an excellent grade point average, defined as an overall 3.0 average throughout the academic year.

OTHER CONSIDERATIONS

You need to identify one to three indicators for each outcome. Each indicator should refer to a different aspect of the outcome, and taken together, the indicators should provide evidence of the outcome as a whole.

As we have seen, for many outcomes, the indicator is obvious and straightforward. The long-range outcome of "Students will graduate from high school" has only one indicator: graduation. But other outcomes require a number of indicators to cover the many dimensions of a concept. Consider, for example, the outcome, "Sixth grade students will develop a habit of reading." What are the indicators of a habit? They may include frequency of independent reading plus a positive attitude toward reading plus an enjoyment factor.

Let's look at another example. An outcome for a family literacy program might be that parents foster a love of reading in their children. Parents who do so have books and other reading materials around the house, are seen reading themselves each day, give books as presents, and read to their children. Any one of these behaviors hints at a love of reading, but two or more of these behaviors better describe it.

Sometimes the gain is not directly observable, so we have to use an indicator that implies the change. In a multicultural reading and discussion program, an interim outcome might be that participants will gain an understanding of and respect for other cultures. A long-range outcome might be that participants will develop a greater sense of community with people of other cultures. There is no easily identifiable behavior that will demonstrate either of these outcomes. Instead, we must identify behaviors that imply the outcomes.

Such behaviors are sometimes called "proxy" or "surrogate" indicators because they substitute for indicators that are directly observable. Fortunately for us, much work in the area of sense of community has been done by educators and sociologists. One indicator of understanding and respect is the ability to explain a custom of another cultural group from the perspective of a member of that group. Some indicators of sense of community are involvement in the community through attendance at functions; membership in or leadership of community organizations; an increased feeling of community satisfaction and pride; and regular, informal mutual assistance and information sharing with others in the community (neighborliness). You will need to use more than one indicator to get a broad perspective. If you are looking for indirect indicators, check with other agencies and groups to see if the indicators (and their data collection instruments, discussed in the next chapter) have already been developed. Keep in mind that you must always adapt the indicators to your specific program.

Another consideration in specifying indicators is the data collection and analysis plan (introduced in the next chapter). Often the approach and timetable for data collection and the type of data analysis that will be required will dictate the exact wording of the indicators, so you will need to revisit and revise the indicators as you work on your data plan.

CONTEXT

It is essential that indicators are decided in the context of your program and community. *Context* refers to the social, political, and economic environment of the community in which your library functions. It is one of the main reasons why you asked other agencies and individuals who interact with your users about indicators when you talked with them earlier about outcomes. If your library participates in a statewide, regional, or national program, a distant planning committee may set outcomes when they design the program. But you must select indicators that make sense for your participants. For example, "increased self-confidence" might be the desired outcome for a national youth program. Based on your knowledge of your community—and with its members' input—you know which of the possible indicators are appropriate and which are not. In some ethnic groups, looking a person straight in the eye might indicate self-confidence; in others it only indicates rudeness. There are wide cultural differences in the use of gestures and body language, too. It's not just cultural differences that affect your choice of indicators; age also makes a difference. For example, behaviors that indicate social interaction among teens are very different from those shown by preschoolers. Your library situation, too, is significant in selecting indicators. An outcome of "increased use of the library" may have in-library use or remote access as indicators, depending on what the library offers and the demographics of the user group. See figure 9 for more on context.

FIGURE 9
Context for Indicators

External influences:

Economic environment (e.g., availability of work, funding level of programs)

Political environment (e.g., supportive of immigrants)

Social environment (e.g., stigma about illiteracy)

Community attitudes toward program

Availability of auxiliary resources (e.g., child care, bus vouchers)

Expectations of funders and other stakeholders

Participants' personal characteristics and status:

Age

Gender

Literacy level

Native language

Educational or employment status

Physical well-being

Emotional well-being

Living arrangements

Economic well-being

Citizenship status

Expectations of program

Quantity and quality of support by family and friends

Library setting in which program is offered:

Library service model

Accessibility for all

Library values, goal, and mission

Attitudes and abilities of staff

Funding sources and certainty

Library's organizational structure

Convenience of program schedule

CASE STUDY

SENIOR INTERNET CLASSES

Part 4

Indicators

We are back at the Anytown Public Library, talking with Yolanda about the outcomes and indicators for the senior Internet classes. The interim outcomes are easy to assess. Since they are changes in skills, staff can observe the participants demonstrating the new skills. The indicators are those demonstrations of skill. For example, senior participants will be able to access the National Institutes of Health senior health web page independently by the end of the first month.

One of the long-term outcomes, intergenerational understanding—for both the teen tutors and the older adult learners—can be tested; if the members of one cohort age group can explain a given situation from the perspective of the other, library staff can assume that understanding has developed. The indicator is the explanation.

But it is far more difficult to select indicators for two other long-range outcomes: friendship and increased self-esteem. Yolanda explains to us that the staff has chosen continuing communication as an indicator of friendship. Communication by e-mail at least once each month during the next six months will be the demonstration of friendship. For the student outcome of increased self-esteem, the staff has chosen two indicators. The first is voluntary participation in a new non-library extracurricular activity during the next six months. The second indicator is a positive change in the student's self-assessment of self-esteem after six months (as compared to a self-assessment done at the start of the program).

TESTING THE INDICATORS

Workform 6, Indicator Selection Criteria, provides a framework for testing your indicators to be sure that they meet all of the criteria just discussed. Another way to test your indicators is to ask this question: "If someone achieved or demonstrated these outcome indicators, would I be willing to say that he or she has achieved the outcome?" If other people, as well as yourself, can confidently respond "yes," then you have selected good indicators. Before you move on to Step 3.2, you should have specified one or more indicators for each of your outcomes.

Step 3.2
Set a Target for Each Indicator

The target is the program's expectation of excellence. In other words, it is the standard of success for the *program*, not the participant. By the time you have finished this step, you should have a well-selected target for each indicator.

TARGETS: THE STANDARD
FOR THE LIBRARY PROGRAM'S SUCCESS

As we have seen, the indicator includes a quantity that defines success for each participant. The target does the same for the library program; it defines the proportion or quantity of participants that must meet an indicator for the program as a whole to be considered successful. Each outcome indicator should have a target, and all targets are numerical and are expressed as either a percentage (proportion or rate) or as a specific number. It is best to use both a percentage and a specific number because either one alone can misrepresent the situation. If a program reports that 100 percent of the participants demonstrated the indicator, it sounds like a very successful program. But what if there were only two participants? Specifying both the percent (100) and the number (2) gives a more realistic picture. A reverse example is a program that reports that 100 participants demonstrated an indicator. Again, this sounds impressive. But if there were 1,000 participants, the less impressive percentage (10 percent) helps round out the picture.

In our earlier job and information center example, one indicator was: "Participant lists four more job options after the program than before." The indicator states the standard of success for the participant. Now we need to add to that a standard of success for the program. A target might be that 70 percent of participants achieve the outcome defined by the indicator. In other words, 70 percent of participants list at least four more career options after the program than before.

But what if only one of the fifty participants can list four more job options? Is the program a success? What if 25 percent of the participants can demonstrate the indicator—is that success? Is the program successful only if 100 percent of the participants demonstrate the outcome? It depends on the local context. Context is how the program functions within the social, political, and economic environment of the community, as well as within the environment of the library. The library's service organization and mission; the attitudes, expectations, and abilities of staff; and the attitudes, expectations, and abilities of users are all components of context. (Refer back to figure 9 for more on context.)

Targets must be set locally, by individual programs, based on their knowledge of the circumstances and the participants. For example, if the job seekers all speak English as their first language, there is a greater chance that all participants will demonstrate the indicator. Another example is that a program with new staff may have different expectations of the participants than the old staff had.

Targets must be based upon experience. So a new program—or a library new to outcome measurement—should not set a target until the first year (or cycle) of the program activity, and the data collection and analysis are complete. The baseline figures from the first year can then be used to select appropriate targets for the next year or cycle.

Baseline information is the most significant factor in setting targets, but it is not the only one. Other factors must also be taken into account when setting targets. These include changes in funding or staffing levels, changes in the program's procedures, and changes in external factors such as demographic characteristics of the user population or changes in the local economy.

Targets should also be reasonable, taking into account the limits of what your program can do. While you don't want to set yourself up for failure by setting unreasonably high targets, you also don't want to set targets so low that staff are not motivated to do their best. Again, experience is very important in setting targets appropriately.

CAUTION

Because indicators and targets must be set locally and based on local experience, it is not wise to use outcome measurement to compare similar programs. This is often a temptation for managers and trustees. If 90 percent of the adult learners at one county library complete their general equivalency diplomas (GEDs), why do only 50 percent complete their GEDs in our county? Shouldn't our library set a target of 90 percent to catch up with the other county? The quick answer is that the communities are different and the educational and language characteristics of the participants differ as well. In fact, the program activities and policies are probably not identical and the staff, of course, is different too. Other significant variations can include the indicator's definition, the data collection instruments and procedures, the data analysis and interpretation, and the time period. Any of these differences can affect your results.

If the library wants to use outcome measures to assess the success of a program, it should compare different years of the same program, or the same program at a different facility or on a different schedule. It should not try to compare across libraries. Similarly, funders should not use outcome data to decide which agencies to fund; this can lead to destructive competition and attempts to skew the data favorably. Target information can, however, be used to identify best practices to continue, and to identify programs that need assistance to meet their outcomes. Another good use of targets is to recognize and celebrate success!

Some evaluators use the terms *outcome verification* or *outcome monitoring* rather than *outcome measurement* to avoid the idea that programs can be compared or even evaluated using outcomes. Instead, the emphasis is on verifying that your program has selected the right goals and outcomes based on community need; has determined the right indicators and targets; and is reaching the destination you were heading for.

Step 3.3
Compose Outcome Statements

Summarizing your selected outcomes, with one to three indicators per outcome, and a target for success in one statement is the final step in Task 3. Pull out Workform 5 from chapter 2; it is the foundation for this step.

You will write one outcome statement for each indicator. An outcome statement, or objective, explains what you expect to happen to a specified number or proportion of your users, as a result of your program, within a specific amount of time. Both the standard for the user (the amount of change or gain) and for the program (the proportion of participants who will achieve the outcome) are included. For example, "80 percent (26) of the new immigrants in the citizenship class will double the number of independent visits to the library by the end of the semester." Note that the outcome statement begins with the user, not the library. Another example begins with the time frame. "By June 2006, 90 percent (100) of the family literacy program participants will double the amount of time they spend reading to their children."

The five components of an outcome statement are listed in figure 10.

FIGURE 10

Components of an Outcome Statement

User/participant

Indicator verb (a measurable action)

Quantity of the action (standard of success for the user)

Number of users who will show the indicator (standard of success
  for the program)

Time frame

Let's return to the job information center example one final time and draft an outcome statement that contains each of the five components for each of the indicators.

> *Interim outcome:* Participants learn of new job or career opportunities
>> *Indicator:* Participant lists four more job options after the program than before the program
>> *Outcome statement:* 70 percent (32) of the job seekers who attend one of the three career opportunity workshops will be able to list four more job options after the program than they could list before the program
> *Interim outcome:* Participants can write a good resume
>> *Indicator:* Participant writes a resume that is rated as good or excellent by the workshop trainer by the end of the workshop
>> *Outcome statement:* 55 percent (25) of the job seekers who attend one of the three resume workshops will write a resume that is rated good or excellent by the workshop trainer

Long-range outcome: Participants will get a job

    Indicator: Participant gets a job within one year of the program

    Outcome statement: 20 percent (9) of the participants who attend all of the programs in the series will get a job within one year of the end of the program

As with the traditional objectives you write for internal program operations or outputs, outcome statements should be "SMART." That is, they should be specific, measurable, attainable, realistic, and time-bound. Check the preceding examples and refer to the components in figure 10 as you draft your own outcome statements using Workform 7, Outcome Statement or Objective. Some sample outcome statements are shown in figure 11.

FIGURE 11
Sample Outcome Statements

By the end of the year, 90 percent (100) of the family literacy program participants will double the amount of time they spend reading to their children each week.

80 percent (26) of the new immigrants in the citizenship class will double the number of independent visits to the library by the end of the semester.

At the end of the hour, 75 percent (15) of the "Introduction to the Internet" workshop participants will access and bookmark two web pages relevant to their selected topic.

85 percent (170) of people receiving books-by-mail will list two benefits the service has provided them during the previous year.

Remember to use one copy of the workform for each indicator. By the time you have finished this step, you should have an outcome statement for each of the indicators for each of your outcomes.

Key Points

The indicator is about the *participant*, while the target is about the *program.*

Indicators and targets must be set locally, based on context.

Each outcome should have one to three indicators.

Indicators are behaviors.

Indicators must include a verb, an object, a quantity, and a time frame.

Indicators must be specific, measurable, observable, and objective.

The indicator, with its outcome, must tell a story.

Each indicator should have a target.

The target must be realistic and based on experience.

Chapter 4

Design the Data Plan

MILESTONES

By the time you finish this chapter you will be able to

- understand the major issues in data collection
- explain the pros and cons of the most common data collection methods
- select the data collection methods that are right for your program
- create or adapt data collection instruments
- decide on data analysis needed
- devise a data plan

NEW VOCABULARY IN THIS CHAPTER

data collection methods	sampling
data collection instruments	data analysis
privacy	coding
confidentiality	qualitative data
repeated measure design	content analysis
validity	cross-tabulation
reliability	

As we discussed in chapter 1, outcome measurement is not scientific or experimental research. We do not have a control or comparison group to compare to our users. Instead, we are looking only at our own program. The building blocks for doing that are changes in individual participants. In other words, we compare each person's level of skill, knowledge, attitude, behavior, or condition before our program with his or her level after the program. In some cases, we also measure the amount of change during the program and a month or longer after the conclusion of the program. But the initial comparison is always of one person's levels over time. The resulting information for each person is then aggregated, or combined, before it is analyzed or interpreted. All outcome information is reported for the whole group of participants. (More on that later.)

Other ways that outcome measurement differs from scientific research are that we are not testing a specific hypothesis, we are not working toward statistical validity, and we are not looking for data to generalize to a larger population or to compare to national results. Instead, we are focused on accurately describing whatever results we find for our users, in the hope that we can use this newfound knowledge to improve our programs. It is often said that evaluations can be used to prove or improve; we are in the latter camp.

You will begin by deciding on a data collection method—or tool—that will best capture your outcomes. Since indicators demonstrate the outcome, you need to find the best way to clearly observe and accurately count the indicators. But before we discuss the pros and cons of specific methods, we need to consider some core issues.

Core Data Collection and Analysis Issues

Six issues need to be considered before designing the data plan.

1. Collecting data should not interfere with the delivery of the service. In other words, library users should not receive less service because of your outcome measurement study. Whenever possible, it is best to include the outcome measurement as part of the service or program, rather than as an additional activity. If it must be a separate activity, try to do it back-to-back with your program. For example, ask your teen technology instructors to stay for pizza and survey them then.

2. Participation in data collection activities such as an interview or survey must be voluntary and not required to receive the service. It is essential to explain this to potential participants. Tell them that they can refuse to answer any one question, or all the questions.

3. Participants' privacy or confidentiality must be respected. Depending on the method you choose, and who actually does the data collection, you might make all participants anonymous. In that case, no names or identifying features are recorded, and the participants' privacy is intact. The disadvantages of keeping all participants totally anonymous are that it is more difficult to link follow-up surveys to earlier ones, and there is no way to analyze responses by demographic or other characteristics. One solution is to link records with specified characteristics (e.g., age) and a unique ID number, but not with names or other clearly identifying information. If you take this route or if you decide that it is necessary to record participants' names or identifying features, all such information should be kept confidential. Confidentiality means that a severely limited number of designated staff or volunteers—that is, those who process and analyze survey results or who

do interviews—know who gave what responses, but that information is not shared with anyone else, even other program staff. All identifiers are removed before anyone else sees the responses. Your privacy or confidentiality policy should be explained to all participants so that they have the chance to opt out of the study if they so choose. And all data collectors and processors—library staff, contractors, and volunteers—should be versed in your privacy or confidentiality policies. The United Way, for example, asks its data collectors to sign a pledge of confidentiality. (You can find its policy and pledge in Tool Kit C, Sample Confidentiality Forms.)

4. The benefits of the data collection activities must outweigh the costs for both the program and the participants. If the staff time necessary to do an outcome measurement study significantly depletes the program's essential activities, or if the time that participants spend on the study seriously reduces their opportunities to receive a service, another method should be chosen. If the program budget is strained severely, or if participants have costs (e.g., extra transportation or child care) related to the study, a source of funding must be sought or a different approach selected.

5. To minimize bias, or even the appearance of bias, the service provider should not serve as the evaluator. In other words, the reference librarian should not interview users about their satisfaction with the reference transaction, and the literacy tutor should not interview students about their experiences in the tutoring sessions. If the data collection is part of the actual service, such as reading comprehension tests during a literacy session, the provider may in fact be the de facto data collector.

6. Data are collected from individuals, but the results are always aggregated and reported as a group. The idea is to measure the outcomes of your service, not to grade an individual's progress. In some instances, such as literacy tutoring, you may be able to do both, but only the composite information is used for outcome reports.

If you'd like to read more about the issues surrounding data collection, see the additional resources on data collection and analysis listed at the back of this book.

TASK 4: DESIGN THE DATA PLAN

Step 4.1
Review Data Collection Methods

As you begin considering which data collection method or tool to use, ask yourself (and your colleagues and staff) the following questions:

What type of information is needed? Factual or subjective? About attitudes or about behavior? What questions need to be answered?

Is this information already available somewhere? If so, who might already have access to much, if not all, of this information?

How standardized must the information be? If some other person or agency has already collected the information, consistency may be an issue. Is that important in your situation? Will you be able to compare it to information you will be collecting later?

How valid (accurate) must the information be? Does the method accurately measure your indicators?

How reliable (consistent) must the information be? Will the method be used the same way by all involved? Would the same data be collected regardless of who collected it, time of day, or location?

Is an instrument (e.g., a test or a survey form) already available? If so, can it be modified for use in your program?

What resources (e.g., expertise, staff time, money) are available to you?

Do you need to collect data before the program and then again afterward? Because outcome measurement is about change, it usually requires pre- and posttesting to demonstrate the change. But that is not always necessary. For example, it is not necessary to do a pre- and posttest if attainment of something new—rather than improvement or increase—is the outcome. In that case, you can work from the assumption that the person did not know the topic or have the skill before the program.

THE SIX MOST WIDELY USED METHODS

Six data collection methods are the most commonly used ones in all types of evaluation, including outcome measurement. These are review of existing records, surveys, tests, interviews, self-reports, and observation by a trained observer. Each has advantages and disadvantages, depending on your situation.

Review of Existing Records

Review of existing records is usually the easiest and least expensive method of data collection. (See figure 12.) Existing records include internal (those of your own program or agency) and external (those kept by others, such as school or employment records) ones. The advantages of this method are that it can have low impact on staff time and can be unobtrusive to participants. Internal program-tracking mechanisms include circulation records, automated log files such as database usage reports, and traditional (manual) attendance logs. Any of these can be used if they are consistently maintained and updated in a timely manner, and if the information can be extracted easily from the system. You may need to ask for consent from the participants; they can give consent in person or virtually by clicking on an "okay" button after reading a confidentiality statement on the web page. Be sure that using this information is in accord with your library's policies as well as with the relevant laws.

External records include those kept by schools, police, parks and recreation, and employment departments. Do official (external) records exist that track your indicator in a way that is useful to you? If so, are the records

FIGURE 12
Review of Existing Records

Advantages:

Inexpensive

Unobtrusive to participants

Disadvantages:

Records may not define terms as you do

Records may not be kept consistently and reliably

Caution:

You may need consent of agency and participant

reliable (i.e., tracked similarly from one individual to another)? Are their definitions of key terms the same as yours? Is the information complete? Is it the information you really need? Note that many records track outputs only and are not related directly to achievement. Can you confirm that the person in their records is the same person as your participant? Is their information consistent enough that you will be able to use it for comparison to data you will collect later? These are important questions, for the major disadvantage of using existing records is that they may not contain the information you really need, or they may not have been kept consistently or completely.

If you think that an outside agency or institution may have some information useful to you, the next question is whether you can get access to those official records. Will the agency share its information? Do you need to get a consent form signed by participants? On this second question, you may need to check with the library's legal counsel. Can you get the records electronically? Another disadvantage of using other agencies' records is that it may be time-consuming to examine others' reports and extract what you need from them. For example, you will probably need to create a checklist or data sheet that program staff or volunteers will fill in from records that others have kept. There also may be ethical or legal considerations if others kept the records; again, you may need to check with legal counsel.

CASE STUDY

TEEN MOTHER TUTORING PROGRAM

Part 2

Existing Records

You may recall that the Anytown Public Library recently decided to measure the outcomes of its successful teen mother tutoring program. An interim outcome for the program's participants, succeeding in school, has two indicators: an improved attendance record and an excellent grade point average.

Unless the library depends on the participants' self-reports, it will need to see school records. So Kathleen, the program director, meets with the school principal, who agrees to release the necessary records for the participants if they sign a release or consent form. She gives Kathleen a copy of the form, which Kathleen then gives to the participants. She explains the outcome study and the need for the school records to each of the teens, all of whom sign the forms. If the participants had been younger, their parents' consent might have been required.

Overall, if you can find out what you need to know without using other agencies' records, and without undue cost and time, it is better to do so. Data that are generated by your own program will definitely take more time initially, but will provide exactly what you need to know without concerns about the quality or timeliness of the information.

Surveys

Surveys are the most popular data collection method used by nonprofit agencies and organizations, according to studies done by the Urban Institute and United Way in 2000. Surveys, also called questionnaires, are best used when you need information from the participant's perspective. They are especially useful for awareness, attitude, and intention indicators.

The advantages of using surveys include the fact that they can be self-administered (form filled in by the participant on paper or online) or asked orally (with answers recorded by someone else if necessary because of language, literacy, or disability issues). (See figure 13.) Surveys allow for anonymity. They are moderate in cost, and are more expensive than using existing records but much less expensive than interviews. Since the survey form asks all respondents exactly the same thing, the responses are more reliable and systematic than other forms of self-report, which means that the results are easy to analyze statistically. Surveys also allow the respondent time to think through the question before answering.

FIGURE 13
Surveys

Advantages:

    Yield user's perspective

    Excellent for awareness, intention, and attitude indicators

Disadvantages:

    Responses may not be accurate or candid

    Language may be an obstacle

    May be difficult to get a 50 percent response rate

Caution:

    The initial creation and testing of the survey form can be expensive

---

Surveys have three major disadvantages. The first is that any information reported by the participant may be inaccurate. For example, asking participants about their knowledge or skill level does not really assess that; instead, surveys measure what the participant perceives to be true. Also, results are often skewed because participants know that they are "supposed to say" that they know more after a program than before.

The second disadvantage is that language can be an obstacle. It is essential to consider whether participants will be able to understand the survey questions, taking into account their age, educational level, and cultural background. Will they be able to accurately answer the questions? Consider self-awareness, knowledge, and language skills. Are your questions neutral or are they written in value-laden terms or overly personal language? Are your questions written in plain and simple English? (For more on wording survey instruments, see Tool Kit D, Tips on Developing Questionnaires.)

The third disadvantage is that it is often difficult to get people to complete and return surveys. Consider what can be expected of your users. How receptive will they be to answering a survey? The response rate for surveys is a serious issue and will vary by distribution method. In other words, a survey sent by mail and returned by the participants by mail has a lower response rate than surveys completed on-site.

In order to get credible results, you need at least a 50 percent response rate to a survey. That is, at least half the people who receive a survey must complete it. Professional statisticians and the federal government require a 75 percent response rate, but for our purposes 50 percent is considered adequate and 70 percent is considered excellent. Take steps to achieve adequate response rates, such as sending an advance postcard or letter, alerting the respondent that a survey is en route; including a cover letter signed by an influential person; keeping the form short and simple; offering an alternative mode such as response by telephone; doing multiple mailings of questionnaires or multiple follow-up phone calls; having program staff encourage users to respond; and providing incentives for completing the questionnaire.

Because outcome measurement is about change, usually measurements (e.g., surveys) must be taken before and after a program or service. The pretest serves as the baseline to which the posttest results are compared. It is assumed that changes in knowledge or skills

EXAMPLE 5

Lawyers in the Library

The Anytown Public Library decides to measure both immediate and intermediate outcomes of its monthly "Lawyers in the Library" program. The program coordinator, Lars, creates a short (half-page) customer satisfaction survey; the last question asks permission to send a follow-up survey by mail three months later. To encourage people to participate, participants are told that all respondents to the customer service survey will be entered in a raffle for a $10 gift certificate to a local independent bookstore. All respondents to the follow-up survey will be entered in a second raffle, this one for a $100 gift certificate.

after the program are likely due—at least in part—to the program. The repeated measure design (i.e., pre- and posttesting) is highly recommended if it is feasible. However, it is not always necessary. When attainment of new knowledge or skills is the anticipated outcome, a pretest is really not needed. For example, if it is clear that the participants have no knowledge of the subject of a class, then testing them before the class is unnecessary.

CASE STUDY

SENIOR INTERNET CLASSES

Part 5

Surveys

A prerequisite of joining Yolanda's senior Internet classes is a lack of knowledge on how to use the Internet. Observation by staff will determine whether the indicator of the interim outcome—that participants will be able to access the National Institutes of Health senior health web page independently—is achieved. There is no need for staff to observe participants early to assess their lack of skill.

Since change in intergenerational attitude is also an outcome, Yolanda will have to survey or interview the seniors' attitudes toward teens (and vice versa) both before and after the series of classes.

Tests

Knowledge or skill tests are the data collection methods most commonly used by educational programs that teach information or skills. (See figure 14.) Many library programs, of course, fit into this category. There are many types of tests: written, oral, and performance. Written and oral tests include multiple-choice questions, completion items, true-false statements, and rating scales.

FIGURE 14
Tests

Advantages:
- Inexpensive to collect and analyze
- High response rate
- Forms may be available

Disadvantages:
- Only appropriate for knowledge or skill outcomes
- Language may be an obstacle

Caution:
- Initial creation and testing of a test can be expensive

Tests have many advantages. The response rate is high because the test is often given as part of the program. In e-learning, for example, there is often a test at the end of each module so that students can check if they are ready to move on to the next section; these tests can also be captured by the instructor and used in outcome measurement. The cost for tests is typically low, as the instructor usually provides the test as part of the curriculum. Tests are widely accepted as credible, and it is easy to analyze their results, which usually are clear-cut and not open to interpretation. Depending on the subject matter, test forms are readily available, so you don't need to create them.[1] Of course, all test instruments must be evaluated for their sensitivity to cultural differences, language, and the needs of people with disabilities (e.g., availability in alternative formats).

Interviews

Interviews, or structured dialogues with an individual participant, are one of the most time-consuming and expensive data collection methods. (See figure 15.) They are labor-intensive, because someone must personally ask each participant questions—either by phone or in person—and the interviews must be recorded, transcribed, and analyzed. Textual analysis of the responses is much more difficult and time-consuming with interviews than with more structured data collection methods such as surveys or tests. But interviews are gold mines when you need information or opinions from the participant's perspective, and they are more systematic than anecdotal self-reports and so are easier to analyze. Note that interviews are, in a literal sense, self-report, but they are considered more objective because the questions are structured in a way that the responses can be compared and quantified once they are analyzed. Interviews are better than a survey for non-native speakers, people with low literacy skills, or people who have difficulties writing. And many people express themselves better and more fully aloud than in writing. For all of these reasons, interviews are often used as adjuncts to a survey, to get more in-depth information on certain issues raised by the survey responses.

Interviews have two more major advantages over all the other methods: they have the personal touch, and they allow the chance to ask follow-up questions for clarification or to pursue unanticipated responses.

All interviews should be done using a structured form with a specific set of questions—including follow-up probing questions that may or may not be asked—so that multiple interviewers receive comparable results that can be analyzed. Caveats for interviews include checking that the participant is comfortable being interviewed and willing to have the interview recorded, and that you have translators as needed. It is essential to train the interviewers to follow the predefined questions systematically, to record the answers accurately and consistently, to use body language to encourage the respondent, and to understand when and how to ask follow-up questions.

Anecdotal Self-Reports

The most common forms of anecdotal self-report are keeping a journal or completing writing assignments about

FIGURE 15
Interviews

Advantages:
  Yield user's perspective
  Allow follow-up questions

Disadvantages:
  Responses may not be accurate or candid
  Labor-intensive
  Expensive to do and to analyze

Caution:
  Interviewers must be well-trained

FIGURE 16
Anecdotal Self-Reports

Advantages:

Inexpensive to collect

Allow participants to express themselves

Disadvantages:

Expensive to analyze

Responses may not be accurate or candid

Language may be an obstacle

Caution:

May be difficult to get users to participate

attitude or behavior changes. (See figure 16.) Open-ended questions on survey forms also elicit self-report. It is the least expensive method of data collection in terms of creating an instrument. Unfortunately, it is also fraught with problems. Because it is by definition subjective, it is not usually accepted as objective and accurate when used on its own. Respondents cannot always recall accurately, and they may not choose to report accurately. But if self-report is just one data collection method among others, it can be a very useful approach to gain a better understanding of how the library program affects participants.

A second major concern with self-report is that not everyone is comfortable doing self-report assignments. In addition to people whose language or writing abilities are limited, people who are self-conscious may not want to participate, and people with disabilities may need an alternative format. All these factors can lead to a poor response rate. Finally, a lot of staff or evaluator time is required to read and analyze all of the written materials that a self-report assignment will generate.

CASE STUDY

SENIOR INTERNET CLASSES

Part 6

Self-Reports

Back at the Anytown Public Library, observation is ongoing to measure an interim outcome of new skills. The long-range outcome of new intergenerational friendships, with the indicator of sustained e-mail correspondence, cannot be observed, however, and requires self-reports. Senior and teen participants are asked to keep a log of their e-mail communications so that staff can tally the number of messages sent and received between the pairs.

Observation by a Trained and Neutral Observer

Firsthand observation of interactions and events is not a commonly used method for outcome measurement, but it is singularly useful in situations where a skill or behavior change is observable. For example, you can watch a reference interview and see the body language of both people. Or you can watch a technology training session and see which participants are able to complete assigned tasks. Observation is sometimes used as an adjunct to another method, as a verification of an indicator measured another way. (See figure 17.)

There are two basic types of observation. Active participation with the user (e.g., tutor with learner) can be considered observation, but most often observation is covert. That is, a neutral and trained person, unidentified to the user, watches an activity. Another variation is overt observation, where the participant is aware that someone is watching as part of an evaluation.

Observation avoids the problems of self-report subjectivity and of low survey response rates, and it is widely considered a valid approach as long as the observers are working from a predetermined guide which specifies who or what to observe, when and for how long, and what to record. Designing a protocol and a reporting form is essential.

The major drawbacks of the observation method are that it is expensive in terms of staff (or volunteer) time and it requires observers to be trained both in what they see and in how they report their observations. It can also raise privacy issues in some sensitive situations, so it is essential to alert users to the fact that they will be observed at some activities (e.g., accessing the library web page). Despite this notification, some users may be uncomfortable if the observer is intrusive. Finally, observation is only appropriate when the indicator can be measured without asking questions; if you must ask questions about an activity or behavior, tests or surveys are better alternatives.

For more information on these six data collection methods, see the additional resources on data collection and analysis listed at the back of this book.

Focus Groups

Note that focus groups are not among the six recommended data collection methods for outcome measurement. Focus groups, which are structured group interviews, are extremely useful when identifying outcomes and indicators because discussion is what you are after. But to assess an individual's progress or achievements, a focus group is not appropriate. You need information on the individual level, not a group response. All of the individual data will be aggregated later, of course, but you must first gather it from each user separately.

Proxy Measures and Limited Interactions

In cases where you cannot use any of the six methods discussed previously, proxy measures can be used for interim outcomes. Often the proxy is an output. If, for example, you are working toward community awareness of the library, you might count the number of hits on the library's website. If you are hoping for increased knowledge on a political issue, you might count the number of pamphlets taken by library users on the issue or the number of people who attend a forum on the issue. Another common proxy measure is intention. For example, at the end of a lecture on healthy lifestyle habits, participants may report that they intend to act on one or more of the speaker's suggestions. Proxy measures should only be used as a last resort for interim outcomes, and should never be used for long-range outcomes.

Outcome measurement, which was originally developed for education and social services, is a special challenge for the limited interactions that characterize much of library service. Think of circulation, information and referral, reference, readers' advisory services, story hours, and guest author speeches. These are all anonymous, short-duration, one-time interactions with users. You cannot count on an opportunity for follow-up, so you will not be able to measure change. One possibility is to use the proxy measure of intention. You can capture it in a brief interview or survey before the user leaves the library. For example, at the end of a reference transaction, you can say, "We are doing an evaluation of library services this week. May I ask you one quick question?" If the person agrees, ask, "What will the information you found enable you to do?" You can get similar information at the end of a lecture by asking people to take a one-minute survey. The question on it can be something like, "How will you apply what you heard today to future activities in your life?" You can also do one-minute entrance and exit surveys, asking a question both before and after a lecture or other program. A variation on this is to distribute a stamped, self-addressed postcard with a one- or two-question survey on it.

Step 4.2
Select a Data Collection Method

The second step in this task is to select the best data collection method (or methods) for each of your indicators. Note that you may want to use more than one method in order to obtain multiple perspectives. For example, you might want to use observation to verify a self-report assignment. Or you might want to use an interview to ask follow-up questions after a survey.

The choice of data collection methods usually requires a weighing of cost, expertise, time required to obtain and analyze the data, and other factors, including participant characteristics and staff preferences. But before you make that final decision, here are three more considerations.

First, the most direct method is usually the one to use. However, there are times when the most direct method is not possible or practical. For instance, the most direct method for measuring changes in behavior is observation, but we cannot observe a behavior that occurs outside the library. Often a less direct record of behavior or even a self-report is the only option. For changes in skills, the most direct method is testing. Again, though, we cannot test for skills that are not applied at the library. So we must often substitute a report by the participant. The participant's account—whether in a survey, interview, or self-report—may tell us more about his or her perception of change than it does about real change, however. For attitude change, the most direct method is self-report or interview. If this is not feasible, observation may be the best alternative.

Next, think about whether your budget can handle the costs of your preferred method. If not, is there a less time-intensive or less expensive way to get the information you need? Data collection costs are both monetary (e.g., printing of surveys, postage, contractual staff) and staff effort (e.g., existing staff time, volunteer time, and expertise). Costs vary greatly by method; number of participants studied; number and types of indicators; frequency of data collection; length of time for which data will be collected; number of data collection instruments involved; availability of existing sources of data (e.g., records); willingness of participants to be involved; degree of data analysis required; and availability of staff time and expertise. To use surveys as an example, the main costs are the development of the survey instrument; printing; postage and staff time for mailing surveys; staff (or volunteer) time for follow-ups by telephone or mail; and data tabulation and analysis.

Unfortunately, little cost information is available. Most of the thirty-five nonprofit agencies surveyed by the Urban Institute in 2000 were not able to provide cost information because they had not treated outcome measurement as a separate budget item. Similarly, most libraries that have used outcome measurement have not tracked it as a separate cost, and so we don't know much about the real cost. In most cases, outcome measurement was closely linked to the service program (e.g., program staff administer pre- and posttests or surveys during initial and final sessions) and little data analysis was done, so the cost was considered negligible. In the same study done by the Urban Institute, some agencies reported costs that came to a per-survey average of $5–6, including the development, printing, and mailing of surveys; and the tabulation and reporting of results.[2] Other experts reported in 1994 that mailed questionnaires typically cost $8–12 per completed survey, and phone interviews can cost $15–20 per interview, including design, administration, and analysis.[3]

Outcome measurement experts estimate that it costs 5–10 percent of a project budget, plus 5–10 percent of staff time, for its first year or cycle.[4] Much of the expense is in contracting with professionals to assist with instrument design, or to do the data analysis. The start-up costs are higher than ongoing costs, because professional development of a data collection instrument or data collection design is relatively expensive.

To reduce the labor costs of outcome measurement, libraries and other agencies can use volunteers (e.g., students in an evaluation course) or contributed time (professionals working pro bono). Mail questionnaires are popular in part because they are less labor-intensive and less expensive than telephone or in-person interviews. Survey forms should be kept simple to improve the initial response rate, reducing the need for follow-up. Simple surveys are also less expensive to tabulate and analyze.

Finally, is the method timely? Will the information be ready when you need it? How long will it take to organize the data collection? How long will it take to gather the information? How long will it take to process the data and analyze the results? When you have sketched out a timeline for your data plan at the end of this chapter, you may find that you need to reconsider the data methods you have selected.

Now that you have reviewed the options, does it seem clear which data collection methods you might want to use? Workform 8, Selecting a Data Collection Method, will help you to select your method (or methods).

Step 4.3
Create or Adapt a Data Collection Instrument

You have selected a method to find out whether your participants demonstrate the outcome indicators. The next step is to formulate how you will employ that data collection method to gather evidence of the indicator. If you've decided to observe participants, what will the observers be watching for? If you've decided to do a survey, what questions will you ask? And what will the observation sheet or the survey form look like? Your data will only be as good as your data collection instrument, so designing (or adapting) it carefully is crucial.

CREATING YOUR OWN INSTRUMENT

When you develop a data collection instrument, you must consider content, language, and format as well as reliability and validity. It is the last two issues that can be the most intimidating for librarians who have no formal statistical training. Remember, we are talking about garden-variety reliability and validity here, rather than statistical validity. Reliability is the dependability and consistency of an instrument. Do you get the same results if the interview is conducted by a different person, or at a different place? Validity is the accuracy of an instrument to measure what it is supposed to. Do the survey questions really measure the change you are looking for? If so, the instrument is said to have credibility.

As for format, look at the structure and the appearance of the instrument. Is it easy to read and easy to answer? Will your participants understand both the questions and how to respond? See figure 18 for questions to consider as you work on the format and wording of the instrument.

FIGURE 18

Evaluating a Data Collection Instrument

Format:

    Is the font clear and large?

    Are the directions for responding clear?

    Does the form have enough space for responses?

    Is the flow of questions logical?

    Are the question-and-answer options or spaces on the same page?

Wording:

    Is the wording easy to understand and free of jargon?

    Is the vocabulary at an appropriate reading level?

    Are the questions written from the users' perspective?

    Are they clear and unambiguous?

    Are they as concise as possible?

    Does each question ask only one thing?

Usefulness:

    Will the answers be useful in improving and promoting the program?

    Will the answers be credible to stakeholders?

    Will the respondent be able to answer accurately?

    Will the respondent be willing to answer honestly?

Another consideration as you develop your instrument is whether to ask users directly about the role the library has played in their achievement of outcomes. Near the end of the survey or interview, after asking about the indicators, some programs ask, "Did our program help you make that change (or gain that skill)?" If the survey uses a scaled question format, this question can be worded as "Please mark the amount to which you agree with this statement: the library program helped me make this change (or gain this skill)." The respondent then selects from the following options: strongly agree, somewhat agree, neutral, somewhat disagree, or strongly disagree. There is disagreement among evaluators about a direct question of this sort, with some evaluators of the opinion that participants will intuit that they should respond "yes" or "strongly agree," so the answers are useless. Others feel that participants, knowing what the program wants to hear, probably will not respond "no" or "strongly disagree," but the differences among "somewhat agree," "neutral," and "strongly agree" still yield useful information. Detailed advice for creating your own questionnaire is given in Tool Kits B and D.

A common mistake of novice evaluators is to ask questions whose answers are not needed. It is almost irresistible to ask about other points of interest while you have the chance, but you should resist. Asking for unneeded information makes your instrument longer, requires more time and effort from the user, and requires more time and effort from the data collector and data analyst. Ask yourself, "For what purpose am I asking this question?" and "How will I use the data?" Use Workform 9, Relevance of Questions in a Data Collection Instrument, to check the relevance of the questions in the first draft of your survey or interview form.

USING AN EXISTING INSTRUMENT

Many survey forms and other data collection instruments are available for use by non-library programs. A local university, the state humanities council, the county education department, or the local United Way or AmeriCorps office all may have instruments for you to use. The creators of some standardized tests and forms charge a fee for their use; others are available at no charge. In all cases, you should obtain permission to use the test or form.

Using another agency or organization's outcome measurement instrument (e.g., survey form) requires careful examination of its relevance to your program and your participants. You will need to adapt it to your situation by editing or adding items. In addition, you need to scrutinize its reliability and validity, just as you would if you developed your own instruments. You must also check its language and format. Again, see figure 18 for questions to help you evaluate a data collection instrument's format, wording, and usefulness.

Consider Using a Web Survey

If appropriate for your users and your program, consider using a web survey. Users are informed, usually by e-mail, that a survey is waiting for them at a specified URL. A hot link to the site is usually given. The user then answers the questions online and clicks on "submit" to return his or her completed survey. Web surveys are increasingly popular because they mean no paper, printing, or postage costs. Often there is little if any survey development cost either, because the companies that host web surveys provide templates. Perhaps the best feature of all, though, is that the host company does the tabulation and statistical analysis too. An Internet search will find you many such companies as well as reviews of some of them.[5] They vary in price (from free to reasonable) and in complexity and features. To summarize, web surveys are easy and inexpensive. However, there are indications that people are already tiring of answering web surveys, so your response rate may be low, and they are only appropriate for users who are comfortable on the Internet.

What Else Do You Want to Know?

Before we leave the discussion of data collection instruments or forms, we have one other important question to consider. What other information beyond indicator achievement do we want to collect from our users? Most survey forms that we fill out ask for basic demographic information such as age, sex, and ethnicity. Often we are asked about where we live and about our household size and income level. Researchers ask for this kind of information so that they can analyze our answers in many ways, to see whether our answers are affected by our age or zip code, for example. Does your program want to collect such information? Note that we do not want to ask anything we will not really use, and we do not want to offend users by asking too many or too personal questions. If your instinct is to say, "let's take this opportunity to collect as much information as possible," please rethink. For every question means more time the user must spend answering, more time the data collector must spend, and more information to analyze by hand or by computer.

However, if you want to investigate the relationships between program success and demographic or other characteristics, you must ask about such characteristics when you collect outcome data. Might it be relevant to see whether older users of the career and job information center achieve the intended outcomes but younger users do not? Or vice

FIGURE 19
User and Program Factors to Consider Using in Data Analysis

User Characteristics:

Age group	Household population
Sex	Household income
Race or ethnicity	Zip code
Primary language	Disability status
Educational level	Employment status

Program Characteristics:

Location of service (e.g., program held at Branch X or at Branch Y)

Delivery of service (e.g., tutoring or training done one-to-one or in a group)

Quantity of service (e.g., one afternoon per week or every afternoon each week)

Length of service (e.g., program in third year or new program)

Personal characteristics of tutors or trainers (e.g., the age of the homework helper or the ethnicity of the technology trainer)

Changes in service (e.g., in policy, funding, or staffing during program time span)

versa? Might we want to know whether middle school children who speak another language at home find the homework help service more or less useful than kids for whom English is their first language? Library and program factors might affect achievement of outcomes, too. For instance, the location, type, and quantity of service a participant receives might affect the outcomes. Think through the most common demographic characteristics of participants and typical program factors (see figure 19) and consider them one by one. Would asking about this particular characteristic provide valuable information for the program? *How* you will analyze the effect of these factors on the outcome measurement data will be discussed later. At this point you just need to decide which questions to add to the data collection instrument.

FIGURE 20
Data Analysis Steps

1. Preparing the data

    Cleaning the data

    Assigning identification tags

2. Coding the data

    Close-ended and quantitative responses

    Open-ended and qualitative responses

3. Processing the data

    Data entry

    Correcting errors

4. Analyzing the data

    Initial calculations

    Basic analysis: frequencies, percentages, averages

    Cross-tabulations

Step 4.4
Decide on Data Analysis Needed

At the end of the data collection period, you will have dozens, hundreds, or even thousands of completed forms. To transform all that data into useful information, it must be analyzed and interpreted. If you have a small number of users and a simple data collection method (such as a short survey), your data analysis needs might also be small and simple. If you are undertaking a more complex outcome study, you may want more analysis. Either way, the types of analysis that your project needs and how it will be accomplished must be decided now; the interpretation will be discussed in chapter 6. Data analysis has four parts: preparing the data, coding the data, processing the data, and analyzing the data. See figure 20 for an overview of the process. For an introduction on how to prepare, code, and process data see Tool Kit E, Preparing, Coding, and Processing Data. Analyzing the data is discussed below.

INITIAL CALCULATIONS

When you have completed preparing, coding, and processing the data and you have an error-free data file for both the pre- and posttest results, it is time to compute the differences between pre- and posttest responses for each participant. You want to find out whether each person demonstrated the indicator—at the level specified in your outcome measurement plan. If your indicator was that "Parents and caregivers who complete the family literacy workshop will report reading to their children twice as often as they had before the workshop," you need to calculate the difference between each participant's answer to the pre-workshop interview question, "How often do you read to your child?" with her answer to the same question after the workshop. All the data analysis will be based on these initial calculations.

DATA ANALYSIS

Data analysis can refer to both descriptive analysis and statistical analysis. Just as the use of outcome measurement in libraries is considered practical research rather than scientific research, outcome data usually need basic, descriptive analysis rather than the more rigorous statistical analysis required by scientific research.

Descriptive data analysis enables us to depict the changes in our users as a whole after the library program or service. It is important to remember that the focus is on the aggregate (or group) of users rather than on any one individual. The most common and basic analysis is the number and percentage of participants who demonstrated the indicator. The number (sometimes called the frequency) is the sum of individual respondents who demonstrated the indicator at the level specified or higher. If the indicator was that all students in the Internet class will print out the first page of two journal articles on their research topic, you count all the students who printed two, three, four, or more articles. You might also add up the number of responses that nearly met the standard, such as how many students provided one article.

These numbers are useful but are not particularly compelling by themselves, since they lack a context. Percentages can provide a context by showing the proportion of participants who demonstrated the indicator. To calculate the percentage, divide the number of people who achieved the indicator by the total number of relevant participants, multiply by 100 (to remove the decimal points), and add the percentage sign. The operative word in these directions is *relevant* because the number that is used for the divisor (or denominator) determines your result. If the indicator specified "teens who attended the entire program," you do not want to use the number of all teens who registered, or the number of teens who came to the first session, but only those who attended the whole program. The percentage is a clear and direct way to express your program's results—and an easy statistic for others to understand. But you always need to report both the number and the percentage because either number alone can be misleading. Twenty percent of 500 participants is quite different from 20 percent of five participants.

If you have set program targets, you will want to see if the program met those targets or not. This means comparing the percentage of participants who demonstrated the indicator against the percentage you had specified in your target. Such information can be very useful in setting targets for the next year or cycle. You will need to plan differently if the target was 50 percent and 85 percent showed the indicator, than if the target was 50 percent but only 25 percent of the participants demonstrated it.

Another basic and useful computation is the average, also known as the mean. It is a popular statistic because everyone knows what *average* means, and it is easy to calculate: you just divide the sum of the scores by the number of participants. If your indicator specifies that participants will earn a certain test score, for example, you may wish to find out the average test score in addition to calculating the number and percentage of people who achieved the indicator. Although 75 percent of participants scored the specified 90 points, you may want to report that the average score of all the participants was 85 points, because that number shows that the average participant came close to the required level of achievement. Averages are important information for any absolute counts (e.g., number of tutoring hours, test scores) and any ratings that have equal intervals between successive values. For example, you may have used a scale asking people to rate their opinion on something from one to five, with one meaning "completely agree," three meaning "neutral," and five meaning "completely disagree." Since the meanings of the rating numbers one to five are evenly spread, the results can be averaged.

Always be cautious about using averages if you have a wide spectrum of scores, though, because one or two extremely low or extremely high scores can easily affect the mean. And keep in mind that the average is not an appropriate summary statistic for every type of data.

If you have used numerals as the codes or names of categories of responses in qualitative or narrative responses, averaging them makes no sense. They are not really numbers but symbols. For example, you may have done a content analysis of the answers to an open-ended question on a test, and assigned the number "one" to represent the repeated theme of transportation and the number "two" to represent schedules. If five responses are labeled "one" and five are labeled "two," averaging them to get the number 1.5 shines no light on the subject. Averages don't work for responses that are categories such as demographic information, either. Whenever a numeral is used as a name for a category, it is best to calculate the most commonly reported rank for each item. (In statistics this is called the mode.) You can find the mode by counting how many respondents gave each answer; the mode is the one given most often.

The mode also applies to answers to ranking questions. For example, you might ask people to rank five aspects of your library program, giving each aspect a number of one through five. Maybe twenty people rank children's services as the highest priority (designated as number one) and ten people rank 24/7 reference as the highest priority, while the other five respondents select one of the other services as their highest priority. There is no need to average these numbers; what is important to note is that children's services was ranked the highest by the most respondents.

The next level of analysis is cross-tabulation. If you want breakouts of the programwide data by demographic or other characteristics (see figure 19), you will want to do cross-tabulations. Cross-tabulations disaggregate (or pull apart) the grouped data to let you look at it by two or more key characteristics. In other words, you can compare findings for subgroups of your respondents to see whom the program most (or least) affected. For example, you can find out whether older participants were more likely to achieve their job and career outcomes than younger people. You can find out if the job seekers who attended workshops weekly were more likely to achieve their outcomes than those who met monthly. You can even see if the older participants who met weekly differed in their outcomes from older participants who met monthly.

Cross-tabulations are very useful, but I must give four caveats about them. First, if you break your users into too many subcategories, you may not have enough people in any one category to make meaningful comparisons. The rule of thumb is that you need at least twenty people in any subcategory. Second, the more comparisons you want to make, the more necessary a computer is to do the analyses. Paper and pencil are cumbersome for large numbers of people and for large comparisons. Third, cross-tabulations only show a correlation among factors and cannot be taken as proof of causation. Finally, from a practical point of view, differences among subgroups of less than 5 percent are not usually meaningful.

If you decide that you do need to determine the statistical significance of the differences between subgroups of participants, either to predict an impact or to generalize from your findings, more sophisticated statistical tests (such as T-tests and chi-squares) will be needed. In this case, your best move is to call in a professional statistician. Keep in mind, though, that the most even a statistician can determine is the probability that the differences (changes) participants have shown are not due to chance. Outcome data by themselves can never prove what actually caused the outcomes.

FIGURE 21

Staff Roles in Data Collection and Analysis

Data manager:

    Select users to study

    Decide on software (if used)

    Code data

    Do (or delegate) accuracy check of database

    Coordinate other staff

    Keep process on schedule

Data collection supervisor:

    Recruit and train data collectors

    Have data collection instruments prepared and duplicated

    Schedule and monitor collectors

    Keep data logs (if used)

    Collect completed forms and deliver to data manager

Data processor:

    Clean data

    Input data

Data analyst:

    Initial calculations

    Basic analysis: frequencies, percentages, averages

    Cross-tabulations

Step 4.5
Devise a Data Plan

Step 5 of Task 4 is to devise the data plan for each indicator. It will pull together your decisions on staff responsibilities, data collection procedures and schedules, and data analysis types and timelines. Use Workform 10, Data Plan, to record your decisions.

STAFF ROLES

Deciding on staff for the roles of data manager, data collector, data processor, and data analyst—or contracting with a firm to fulfill those roles—should be done up front. (See figure 21.) Start by identifying the data manager or coordinator. The person providing the service being measured should not be asked to be the data manager: this prevents both bias and burnout. (But the provider will be asked to contribute to the interpretation of the data, as discussed in chapter 5.) The data manager will spend approximately 5–10 hours per week during data collection and analysis.[6] The data manager should be a good supervisor, and be detail-oriented and careful. This person is responsible for keeping the data collection and analysis moving smoothly and on schedule. He or she will make decisions on which users to study and which data management software programs (if any) are used. The data manager will also prepare and code the data before it is entered and will check the completed database for accuracy (or supervise others in doing so), as well as supervise the data processor and the data analyst. Most important, the data manager must appreciate how essential the data analysis is to provide meaning to all of the work preceding it. Because of that understanding, he or she will allot the necessary amount of time and attention to see that it is done well.

A second staff member may be asked to take the role of data collector (or data collector supervisor, if there will be multiple collectors). In smaller libraries, though, the roles of data manager and data collection supervisor may be combined. The data collection supervisor is responsible for recruiting and training data collectors, if necessary, as well as scheduling them and monitoring their work. He or she will assign someone to duplicate the instruments and will be responsible to collect the completed forms for the staff member who needs them next—the data processor. This is usually a support staff member who is experienced with spreadsheets and databases.

The fourth staff member who will handle the data is the analyst. Every library has at least one staff member who loves crunching numbers, and that's the person for this role. Often it is the person responsible for compiling the statistical report for your state library agency to submit to the Federal-State Cooperative System for Public Library Data for the National Center for Educational Statistics, but it may be an administrative assistant to the director or the head of technical or IT services.

WHICH USERS WILL YOU STUDY?

The next decision to make is whether you will survey/interview/test all of the participants in your program. If you have less than 100 participants, it is best to include them all. If that is not possible—or you have a larger group—you may want to collect data on only a sample. If you decide to use a sample, select the names now. (For information on sampling methods, see Tool Kit F, Sampling.)

DATA COLLECTION PROCEDURES

It is essential to codify all the policies and procedures—such as how and where data is collected—so that everything is done systematically and uniformly. The data manager, working with the data collection supervisor if you have one, must monitor and track the data collection process. This may include keeping a record of data collection for each participant. How many times has the person been contacted? When were any consent or confidentiality forms returned? Which staff members have handled the data (i.e., data collectors, data processor, and analyst) and when?

There are many details to work out for each data method used. For example, if you have decided to use a survey, created in-house or adapted from elsewhere, will you administer the survey by mail? If so, be sure to include a standardized cover letter and a stamped self-addressed envelope for users to return the survey. No matter the format, if the response rate to your survey is not acceptable, what kinds of follow-up will you do to encourage more people to respond? A second survey form? A postcard or e-mail reminder about the survey? Or will you ask users to complete the survey in-house? If reading or understanding English is a barrier, will you offer a staff member or volunteer to read or translate the survey for the user?

If you have selected interviews as your method, will you do the interviews by phone? Exactly how will this happen? When and where will the calls be made? Telemarketers do phone interviews so commonly now that many people have "phone survey fatigue." Will you offer an incentive for participating? Have you left an opportunity for a participant to decline? Or will you interview in person? Do you have translators available if necessary? How will you meet the special needs of people with disabilities? If you have decided on tests, how and where will they be given? What about observations?

Don't forget that for all types of data collection, you need to have a privacy policy and a procedure for sharing it with participants. And in some situations—especially when children are involved—you may need to have signed consent forms. Who will make these decisions? Who will carry them out?

DATA COLLECTION SCHEDULE

You probably will need to collect pre-program data so that you can document changes after the program. Will you do this at the beginning of the program itself or beforehand? What data collection schedule will give you the most significant information on interim outcomes? Monthly? Annually? At the end of each program cycle? What about long-range outcomes? Long-range outcome data are typically collected approximately two years after a participant enters or completes a program. To see whether changes are sustained, you will need to do a follow-up study at least six months after the participant leaves the program or has done the "post" part of the outcome measurement. It is important to develop a comprehensive schedule that includes the data collection needs at every stage of the process. It is relatively easy to schedule data collection during or immediately after a program. It is more difficult to plan to collect data prior to the start of a program and even more difficult to remember to collect data a year or two after a program, when you have moved on to new programs and services.

Key Points

Collecting data should not interfere with a participant's ability to receive services or with his or her privacy or confidentiality.

Data are collected from individuals, but the results are always aggregated and reported as a group. The idea is to measure the outcomes of your service, not to grade an individual's progress.

The right data collection method for your program is the one that best captures your indicators, is as direct as possible, fits within your budget and your staff's expertise, is culturally sensitive and timely, and will provide credible information.

Outcome measurement is not scientific research and requires descriptive analysis, not statistical analysis.

Without data analysis, all the work of data collection is wasted.

Analysis cannot prove what actually caused the outcomes.

Results should not be compared to the results of other programs unless the programs and the evaluation were designed and managed together.

The outcomes reflect the library's contribution to a goal, but they cannot be attributed to the library program alone.

Notes

1. One website that describes and links to tests (and survey instruments) is the Educational Testing Service's *Test Link: The World's Largest Test Collection Database,* www.ets.org/testcoll/index.html. It describes 20,000 tests and where to obtain them. It also has 1,000 tests that are available for purchase from ETS via the site. Another useful website is the University of Nebraska at Lincoln's *Buros Institute Directory of Mental Measurements,* http://buros.unl.edu/jsp/search.jsp. It lists 4,000 commercially available tests in eighteen subject areas. Half of these tests have been reviewed by them and the reviews are available for purchase on the website.

2. Elaine Morley and others, *A Look at Outcome Measurement in Nonprofit Agencies* (Washington, DC: Urban Institute, 2000).

3. Joseph S. Wholey and others, *Handbook of Practical Program Evaluation* (San Francisco: Jossey-Bass, 1994).

4. Jane Reisman and Judith Clegg, *Outcomes for Success!* (Seattle, WA: Evaluation Forum, 2000), 56; Sally Bond and others, *Taking Stock* (Chapel Hill, NC: Horizon Research, 1997), 37; W. K. Kellogg Foundation, *Evaluation Handbook* (Battle Creek, MI: W. K. Kellogg Foundation, 1998), 54.

5. Reviews of web survey software and host companies appear in *PC Magazine, PC World,* and other consumer magazines for computer users. A partial list of online survey hosts is available at http://www.albany.edu/cpr/gf/resources/survey-tools-online.html, and on the pricing page of http://www.surveymonkey.com. Gail McGovern, an independent library consultant in Sacramento, California, brought these resources to my attention.

6. Hatry and others, *Measuring Program Outcomes,* 13.

Chapter 5

Prepare for Implementation

MILESTONES

By the time you finish this chapter you will be able to

- complete your outcome measurement plan
- respond to staff concerns
- design data collector training
- pilot-test data collection and analysis
- design an action plan for outcome measurement

NEW VOCABULARY IN THIS CHAPTER

outcome measurement plan

logic model

pilot test

action plan

By now you are impatient to get started collecting and analyzing information from your participants, but you have one more task ahead of you. It is essential to prepare staff and write an action plan so that everyone is on the same page and schedule. Now is also the time to test your data plan, so that all will run smoothly when you implement it.

TASK 5: PREPARE FOR IMPLEMENTATION

Step 5.1
Write an Outcome Measurement Plan

As you worked through the tasks and steps in the first four chapters of this book, you have identified each element of an outcome measurement plan. The information in your completed Workform 10 (Data Plan), Workform 7 (Outcome Statement or Objective), and Workform 5 (Inputs, Outputs, and Outcomes) together make a complete outcome measurement plan. Using those forms, fill in Workform 11, Outcome Measurement Plan, so that most (if not all) of those pieces are combined into one document that represents your best thinking and decisions. Some programs present the outcome measurement plan in a graphic form, called a logic model. (See figures 22 and 23.) Note that this *outcome measurement plan* is conceptual rather than operational. The implementation plan comes later.

Step 5.2
Address Staff Concerns

Although you have become immersed in outcome measurement, your colleagues, program staff, and volunteers may be ambivalent or even hostile about trying a new type of evaluation. They may see outcome measurement as just another "flavor of the month" planning and evaluation approach, one that they will be required to do this cycle or this year and will never use again. They might think of outcome measurement as another added-on task and more paperwork when they are already overstretched. They might be concerned about their own lack of evaluation or statistical skills. They may feel that they are being asked to take responsibility for outcomes over which they have little control. They may worry about whether the results will be used for unfair comparisons to other departments or libraries. Or they may fear that their jobs will be vulnerable if the selected outcomes are not met. All of these concerns are valid and must be addressed by you and by the members of the management team.

Any change can cause stress for people, and outcome measurement definitely is a change. Participants in workshops on outcome measurement report that the most difficult part of the process is coming to terms with the radical paradigm shift from focusing on what we do to focusing on the benefits for the users. If there is too much stress around implementing outcome measurement, the workforce (staff and volunteers) will be resentful, resistant, and ineffective.

FIGURE 22
Sample Logic Model: Institute of Museum and Library Services

(Organization Name)

(Influencers)

(Mission Statement)

(Program Name)

(Program Purpose)

We do what:

To whom:

For what outcome:

(*Cont.*)

Source: This outcome measurement logic model, distributed to state library agencies by the Institute of Museum and Library Services, was created by Claudia B. Horn of the Alliance Group, LLC, for the IMLS in 2000.

FIGURE 22 (*Cont.*)

_____
(Program Name)

(Program's Services)

(Program's Services)

(Program's Population)

(Program's Admission Criteria—optional)

(*Cont.*)

FIGURE 22 (*Cont.*)

(Program)

Outcome #1

Outcome's Indicators

Data Sources

Applies to

Target

Data Intervals

(*Cont.*)

FIGURE 22 (*Cont.*)

_____
(Program)

_____
_____
_____

Outcome #2

Outcome's Indicators

Data Sources

_____
_____
Applies to

Target

_____
_____
Data Intervals

FIGURE 23
Sample Logic Model: California State Library

LSTA Outcome Measurement Project Design

Library:_____

Project Name: _____

Users: _____

Services/Programs

What will the library provide to the user in order to address the user need and
move toward the library goal?

Inputs

What resources will the library use to provide the services/ programs?

Outputs

How many of each service/program will we provide? How many users will be served?

Intermediate Outcome(s)

\What is the short-term benefit to the user as a result of the program/service?
What will the user do that is necessary if he or she is to achieve the long-term outcome?

(Cont.)

Source: This outcome measurement design form was created by Carla Lehn, literacy consultant at Library
Development Services of the California State Library (CSL), and Rhea Rubin in 2002. It has been revised and
is currently used for both designing and reporting by all outcome measurement projects funded by the CSL.
The current version is on the CSL website at http://www.library.ca.gov.

FIGURE 23 *(Cont.)*

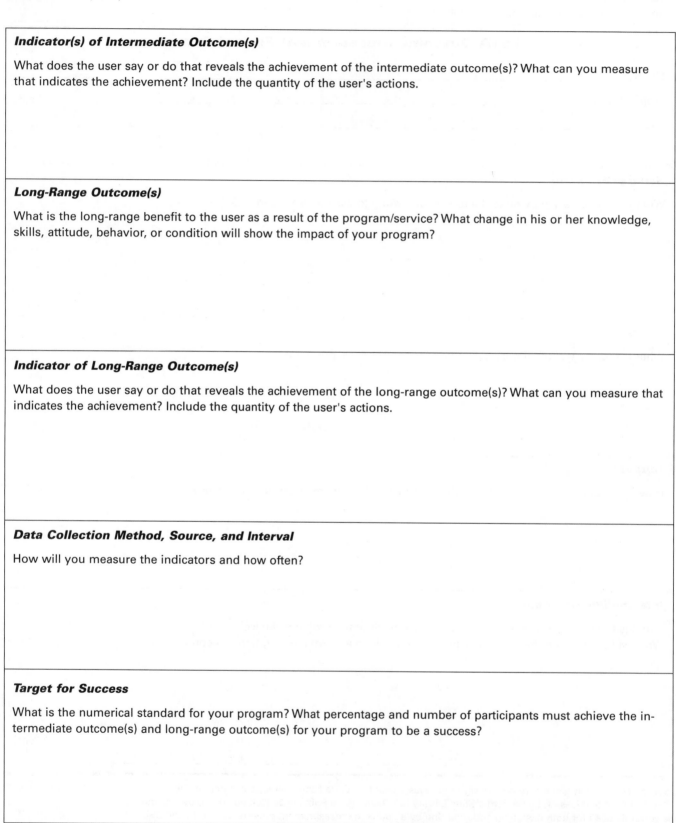

Indicator(s) of Intermediate Outcome(s)

What does the user say or do that reveals the achievement of the intermediate outcome(s)? What can you measure that indicates the achievement? Include the quantity of the user's actions.

Long-Range Outcome(s)

What is the long-range benefit to the user as a result of the program/service? What change in his or her knowledge, skills, attitude, behavior, or condition will show the impact of your program?

Indicator of Long-Range Outcome(s)

What does the user say or do that reveals the achievement of the long-range outcome(s)? What can you measure that indicates the achievement? Include the quantity of the user's actions.

Data Collection Method, Source, and Interval

How will you measure the indicators and how often?

Target for Success

What is the numerical standard for your program? What percentage and number of participants must achieve the intermediate outcome(s) and long-range outcome(s) for your program to be a success?

It is best to directly acknowledge that outcome measurement means change, even if only for a specific program and a distinct amount of time. Have a meeting of all staff members and volunteers who will be involved. This includes managers, support staff, and information technology staff, as well as program staff. Discuss the reasons for trying outcome measurement and stress the benefits of this type of measurement for the library. Have managers talk about how outcome measurement fits in with the library's mission and goals, and answer any other "why" questions from staff. Involve everyone in a discussion of how outcome measurement can be implemented with the least disruption in work schedules and responsibilities. Later in this chapter you will design an action plan that should help those who have questions about "who" is to do "what" "when." If people still have concerns about the workload or timetable, directly address the issue of what other work must be postponed or which other staff will pick up tasks, and be realistic about what can be done.

Offer training in outcome measurement for anyone who wants to learn more. Offer empathy and technical assistance to anyone who is assigned a task that is new to them. Some questions may be unexpressed or harder to address. So keep the lines of communication open, share information regularly, and do nothing in secret, which can result in worry and suspicion. Instead, ask everyone for input into the development of the action plan (the last step in this task). And as outcome measurement is implemented, allow opportunities for people to talk and to share their concerns. As with any other new initiative, be forthcoming with praise and gratitude, and reward people for good work as soon and often as possible. Use each milestone as an opportunity for discussion, troubleshooting, and celebration.

Step 5.3
Recruit and Train Data Collectors

The best data collection is integrated into the program itself. That way, it is less intrusive for participants and is less of a burden on them and on library staff. For example, adult learners in a literacy program are accustomed to both interviews and reading tests as part of their program. People of any age learning a computer-based skill are used to having pop-up quizzes as part of the course design. This means you may be able to do outcome measurement without additional staff. However, it is important that you avoid using the direct provider of the program as the evaluator in order to avoid any appearance of bias. One solution is to have a literacy tutor, for example, interview someone else's learner and vice versa. The instructor of one computer class can test the students of another teacher's class and vice versa. Another solution is to have a manager or a support person from your department do the interviewing, testing, or observation.

But depending on the program you are going to use for outcome measurement, the number of participants, and what type of data collection method you have selected, you may need other or additional people to be data collectors. Note that the fewer data collectors the better, so that there is a greater chance of consistency in how information is recorded. If you need to find collectors, consider staff from other departments, members of the library's Friends group, or members of the board who can serve as data collectors. Perhaps you can afford to pay students or retired people to do this work. If none of these ideas work, it may be necessary to recruit volunteer data collectors. This can be a challenge, though most communities have a volunteer center that can help you. If your library already uses volunteers in other capacities, you may want to recruit from that list. Another possibility is to recruit college students who can get class credit, or work-study credit, for helping with a community study.

Unless your own program staff can do the data collection, it is wise to develop a job description for data collector and use it to recruit people. As in all volunteer management, a job description allows you to select exactly the right volunteers who have the necessary credentials. It allows the volunteers to understand what is expected of them and what they are promising to do. It serves as an agreement and the basis for supervision. And if the person proves unsuitable for the job, it gives the grounds for dismissing the volunteer. See figure 24 for a sample job description for data collector.

The training of data collectors should begin with an explanation of why the library staff decided to use outcome measurement and how they foresee using the information that is gathered during the process. All data collection instruments must be discussed, including their purposes and the procedures for using them. Next, the collectors should

---

FIGURE 24
Sample Data Collector Job Description

Data collectors are needed for the period of January and February 2006. They will be administering both in-person and telephone interviews with users of the Job and Career Information Center. The information gathered from these interviews will assist the library in improving services.

Qualifications:

- Minimum age of 18
- Good attention to detail
- Good listening skills
- Ability to read, write, speak, and understand English
- Ability to write legibly

Reports to: Program Manager, Central Library

Responsibilities:

1. Attend and successfully complete one 2-hour training, provided by the library free of charge, and held at the central library in December.
2. Sign up for a minimum of two 2-hour shifts per week during January and February.
3. Come to the library on assigned dates and times to do interviewing in-person and by phone. All work will be done at the library.

4. Maintain confidentiality of all information about the interviewees given by the library or the interviewees themselves. Volunteers will be required to sign a confidentiality pledge.

Other Notes:

1. All work will be done at the Central Library during the hours of 9:00 a.m.–11:00 a.m. or 6:00 p.m.–8:00 p.m., Monday through Friday.
2. Some volunteers will be asked to assist in pilot-testing the data collection. This includes participating in a debriefing session after the pilot-test.
3. Volunteers will use a structured interview form to ask the questions and record the answers. These forms are the property of the library and must be submitted at the end of each shift.

Length of Commitment: Two months

Grounds for Dismissal: Failure to carry out assigned responsibilities as directed; breach of confidentiality

Contact Person: Jerry Tallchief, 987-6543

Source: This volunteer job description concept and sample are based on Carla Campbell Lehn, *Volunteer Involvement in California Libraries: Best Practices* (Sacramento: California State Library, 1999).

practice using the appropriate instruments in mock interviews, record extractions, or observations. Any relevant policies—for example, confidentiality—must be detailed and forms signed. During the training, any person who appears ill-matched for this work should be dismissed.

Step 5.4
Pilot-Test the Data Plan

This step includes pilot-testing the data collection instruments (e.g., questionnaire, observation checklist), the data collection procedures, and the data analysis. Every person who will be involved in data collection or analysis should be part of the pilot-test. This means clerical support staff, information system staff, and managerial staff, as well as the data collectors. Arrange for the pilot-test—which should last as long as it takes to span all the data collection and analysis activities—to be held in conditions as close to the actual administration conditions as possible.

This is a trial run of your entire data plan. You should implement all parts of your system, just as you will in the actual implementation of outcome measurement. This provides an invaluable opportunity to discover additional outcomes, poorly defined indicators, cumbersome data collection and analysis procedures, and reporting problems. Finding them out now means you can fix the problems and ensure that the process runs smoothly in the actual implementation.

If you are going to study a sample of your participants, select a sample for the pilot-test to see if your selection method works. If you will require data collectors to enter the responses to their interviews into a spreadsheet, this is the time to see if they understand how to do it and if the spreadsheet is set up correctly. If a supervisor will be monitoring the data collectors, does he or she have an appropriate logbook or form? Are all of your policies—including confidentiality—reflected in the procedures that staff are using?

Pilot-testing also gives a clear picture of what your data collection and analysis requires in terms of staff or volunteer time, as well as other resources such as postage and telephones. For example, if you are doing a mail survey, you can discover the response rate on the first mailing and see what type and how many follow-ups are necessary to get an acceptable response rate. If you are extracting information from records, you can find out how much of the data is available or missing. If you are doing telephone interviews, you can discover the refusal and callback rates. If you are using observers, you can discover when and why observations cannot be completed. All this information will provide a much more realistic idea of what the "real" data collection will be like. In the data analysis area, you can see how much time it takes to tabulate and enter the data, to analyze narrative data, and to run the tabulations and cross-tabulations.

You might decide that you want to ask for the same information from your data collectors throughout implementation, so that the data manager can monitor how the process is working and catch any problems as they arise.

PILOT-TESTING THE INSTRUMENTS

To pilot-test a survey or interview instrument, have two or three reviewers use the instruments with six to twelve participants who are representative of the people you will be surveying or interviewing. For example, if you will be surveying people with limited

English skills, be sure to test the forms on people with limited English skills. Inform the participants that this is a pretest and that you will be debriefing them later; set up a time to do that. Ask them to keep track of the amount of time it takes them to complete the survey. If this is a telephone interview or survey, the data collector should note the start and end times on the form and also record how many phone calls it took before the actual interview or survey happened. To test a record extraction form, collect data from five to ten records and have two or three reviewers extract the information from the same records; then compare their completed forms to see if they are consistent across reviewers. As with the interview forms, have the data collector note the start and end time on each record extraction form. For trained observer ratings, ask three to five raters to observe and rate the same five to ten behaviors in the same settings, noting the start and end times. Again, compare their completed forms to see if observers apply the criteria consistently.

In debriefing participants after questionnaires, ask first what they think the survey is about. Then ask about the wording of the questions. For example, were any questions confusing or difficult to answer? Do they think other people will have trouble understanding any of the words that were used? Did any of the questions seem too personal? Did any of the questions make them feel uncomfortable? Next ask about the adequacy of the response categories—were there the right number of choices? If it was a form that respondents filled in themselves, was it easy to use? Were the directions clear? Were the layout and format okay? How long did it take to complete the survey? Were they told about the confidentiality policy? Ask also whether the interviewer was respectful and patient to see if the data collectors need more training.

Conduct a similar debriefing of the data collectors, asking them whether the participants were hesitant about being surveyed or interviewed. If so, why? Did the participants have difficulty understanding or answering any questions? Did the vocabulary seem appropriate? Did any questions seem offensive or off-putting? Were there enough response categories, or did you have to add some? Was the survey or interview too long? For example, did the respondents seem engaged throughout or were they losing interest? Was the ordering of the questions correct? That is, did they flow in a logical manner? Did you experience any difficulty or confusion yourself during the survey or interview? Were you asked any questions you were not prepared to answer? How long did it take to complete each interview? Finally, look at the data collectors' completed forms. Did they have enough space to write? Are there any indications of difficulty using the form?

If the participants filled in forms themselves, look carefully at the answers. Did people follow the directions correctly? Did they have enough space to write? Are there any indications of difficulty using the form?

The staff or volunteers who will tabulate and analyze the results should look at both the forms respondents filled in and the ones that collectors completed. Can they use the information elicited on the forms? Is the information recorded in a consistent enough way despite different people using the forms? Are there other questions we should be asking to get the information we'll need for the analysis? Does the content or the layout need revision to make the forms easier for tabulation or analysis? If the data collectors are entering information into a spreadsheet or other software program, are they doing so correctly and consistently? Is the software program you are using powerful enough for your number of participants and questions?

Step 5.5
Design an Action Plan

One reason that library programs often shy away from program evaluation is that they overestimate the amount of work it will be. Ironically, when libraries do decide to evaluate, they typically underestimate the staff time involved. An action plan makes the conceptual data plan operational. While designing the action plan, program staff have to estimate what each activity requires in terms of time and staffing. This should prevent unpleasant surprises later on. Use Workform 12, Action Plan, to develop your action plan.

The pilot-testing you have just done informs this implementation plan. Studies suggest that 10–20 percent of program resources (including staff) are necessary for evaluation. Of course, the amount of resources needed depends on your data plan: the number of participants to be studied, the length of time for which data will be collected, the number and type of data collection instruments, the availability of existing sources of data, the difficulty of administering the data collection, and the types of data analysis. Considering the many uses of the information you will gather—in terms of accountability, program improvement, resource allocation, and marketing—the cost is an appropriate investment.

Although the action plan is primarily to ensure that the outcome measurement process happens in a reasonable time frame, and that staff members are given the necessary time to complete each assignment, the plan also serves the purpose of helping with staff concerns. Staff members who are reluctant to try outcome measurement see exactly what they are expected to do, broken into manageable steps. They also see when each part of the process is to happen. If the time allotted is insufficient, or the project is behind schedule, they can and should discuss the issue with their managers.

One aspect of the action plan that is often omitted is quality control. You should have regular meetings to check in with data collectors and analysts to identify problems and elicit suggestions. As you monitor the data collection and analysis, you are sure to notice kinks in the system that can be resolved the next time. If it is any consolation, the first time data is collected and analyzed is always the most difficult and the most expensive.

Key Points

Staff and volunteers need information and clear, open communication.

Use a job description to ensure that the right people do the data collection.

Training of data collectors is essential.

Pilot-testing of both data collection instruments and procedures exposes problems before the real implementation.

An action plan provides comfort to reluctant staff members and a safety net for you.

Chapter 6

Make the Most of Your Results

Many programs collect outcome data but waste all the time and effort spent—they never use their results. A study by the Urban Institute in 2000 found that only 44 percent of the agencies surveyed used their results for program improvement and only 28 percent used them for fund-raising.[1] Few reported their results to other staff members, users, or volunteers. That's not to say that someone in the agency didn't write a report—which was often a requirement of funding—but that the report was a dead end.

In the nonprofit world, the term *outcome measurement* is giving way to the term *outcome management* precisely to express that measurement is only one aspect of the process, and that the post-analysis use of outcome information should not be neglected. A symposium in 2002 focused on the interpretation and uses of outcome information, particularly to improve services. The thirty nonprofit organizations that participated identified five factors that facilitate the use of outcome information:

- supportive management and organizational climate
- availability of funding
- staffs' perception of the validity of the outcome information
- level of proficiency at collecting outcome information
- use of current technology for data processing and analysis[2]

Do you have one or more of these assets available to you? Since you have invested so much in the outcome process already, why not make the most of your results? The information in this task will give you some ideas about how to do that.

TASK 6: MAKE THE MOST OF YOUR RESULTS

Task 1: Select a Program for Outcome Measurement

Task 2: Determine the Interim and Long-Range Outcomes

Task 3: Make Outcomes Measurable

Task 4: Design the Data Plan

Task 5: Prepare for Implementation

Task 6: Make the Most of Your Results

    Step 6.1: Interpret your results

    Step 6.2: Communicate your results

    Step 6.3: Use your results to move forward

Step 6.1
Interpret Your Results

"Data do not speak for themselves. We must go beyond calculating outcomes to interpreting them."[3] Chapters 4 and 5 discussed collecting data and analyzing them, manipulating raw data into intelligible numbers and, in the case of percentages and cross-tabulations, providing some context for the numbers. But you were still left with a sheet or more of numbers without explanations. At this point it is time to interpret the data, which means making sense of your findings and drawing conclusions.

It is important that all interpretation is based on even-handed and cautious judgments. Because the same information can be interpreted in many ways depending on an individual's knowledge and bias, you need to involve program staff and volunteers in discussing the meanings of your numbers. In some instances, when you are confounded by one or more result, you may need to convene a focus group of users to help you understand unexpected results.

First, create visual presentations of your findings such as charts, tables, and graphs. These can be simple and hand-drawn for in-program or in-library use only. Looking at the results in a graphic form allows you to see connections you might have missed, and will help the others involved in interpretation to see the findings clearly. You might also collate any textual responses that you want discussed, and gather insightful comments and anecdotes. All of this preparation for interpretation will be useful, too, when you write your reports.

Next, distribute the numbers, the graphics, and any other information to direct service providers and other staff and volunteers whose perspectives will contribute to the interpretation. Invite them to a small group meeting for discussion of the outcome findings and ask them to study the information first. If you have been working in collaboration with another organization or agency, you may want to include representatives of those groups in the meeting, too. (If you prefer not to hold a meeting you could ask for comments by e-mail or hand, but a group discussion will usually yield more ideas and a multilayered interpretation.) At the meeting you want discussion of both the expected and unexpected results. Possible questions include:

> Which findings surprise you and why?
>
> Does the number of people who demonstrated the indicator seem unusually high or unexpectedly low?

CASE STUDY

SENIOR INTERNET CLASSES

Part 7

Interpreting the Data

It is now seven months after the conclusion of the first cycle of senior Internet classes. At the last session, the senior participants had been observed using their new skills, and their achievement of the interim outcome of skill acquisition was clear. After six months, Yolanda and two volunteers contacted both the seniors and the teens to see whether the long-range outcomes had been achieved. Intergenerational understanding, the first long-range outcome, was achieved by more than the target amount. But the friendship and self-esteem outcomes were not clear. Yolanda calls a meeting to discuss the data.

She invites the teen and senior representatives on her planning committee, the instructor, the two volunteer data collectors, an adult services librarian, and the young adult librarian. Over cookies, she shares the data that has been collected on the friendship and increased self-esteem indicators. Approximately 20 percent of the senior and teen participants have reported that they are in e-mail communication with their partner, the indicator of friendship. The target had been 80 percent, so Yolanda is looking for an explanation of the unexpectedly low number. The teen representative mentions that teens prefer instant messaging to e-mail. The senior representative suggests that senior participants do not necessarily check and answer e-mail messages regularly. A librarian points out that the seniors may not even have e-mail service at home; they came to the class to learn to use the Internet and they do so at the library. The volunteer data collectors report that both seniors and teens seemed surprised to be asked about their e-mail contact. The instructor explains that none of the participants had been coached to keep up their e-mail correspondence. After much discussion, the group agrees that the low proportion of participants demonstrating the indicator may be due to the simple fact that they did not think of communicating after the class and that the missed target may be due to lack of clear instructions for the participants. The problem is in the data collection. Though she doesn't like the idea of "teaching to the test," the instructor agrees that she should suggest e-mail communication to the participants in the next cycle.

Next Yolanda asks about the self-esteem outcomes for the teens. One indicator—a positive change in the student's self-assessment—was demonstrated by 90 percent of the teens. But only 5 percent demonstrated the other indicator, a new non-library extracurricular activity. The group discusses many possible factors for this, including the teens' busy schedules, their lack of transportation, and the large amount of homework they have. Soon the conversation focuses on the fact that this indicator may be off-base. Joining extracurricular groups may not indicate increased self-esteem, and not joining may not demonstrate low self-esteem. The problem is in the indicator. Yolanda moves the discussion onto other, better indicators to use next time.

Are there categories of users for whom the outcomes were not as successful as anticipated?

Looking at the cross-tabulations, which user characteristics seem to be correlated with unexpected results? Any ideas why? Are certain participant characteristics associated with a higher level of outcome achievement?

Which program characteristics are correlated with unexpected results? Any ideas why? Are certain service delivery modes or locations associated with a higher level of outcome achievement?

What other factors might be affecting the results? Internal factors such as sudden staff turnover? External factors such as changes in public transportation?

Have the data collection methods in any way contributed to unusual or unexpected responses? Was the timeline or the target unrealistic?

Be sure to compare your findings with any assessment information from other time periods or cycles. Are the findings on an upward or downward trend? If the library has made any significant recent changes, compare your findings from before and after the changes. Consider other events (inside or outside the library) that may have affected your findings. Compare your results with the program's targets. If the number is way off from the target, why do you think you selected a target that was too high or too low? According to the Urban Institute study, only 14 percent of the agencies surveyed compared their outcome data to targets set earlier, and only 35 percent compared outcome levels over time.

You want to look especially hard at responses to open-ended questions in interviews and on surveys. They may include commentary on why something did or did not happen. They may also list unanticipated outcomes deserving of another cycle of measurement to see how widespread they are. Besides looking at the most common answers, consider the minority responses. What do they suggest?

Disappointing outcomes and unexpectedly good outcomes both deserve special scrutiny, because explaining them can lead to important program or data collection modifications. If you are unable to explain them, do a group interview with participants or have a more detailed analysis done by a professional statistician.

Step 6.2
Communicate Your Results

This step encompasses disseminating interpreted results both internally and externally. Internal communication refers to sharing information with program staff and volunteers, other library staff, and library management. External communication is to library users, the library board or commission, partner agencies, the general public, funding agencies, and local government.

First you must decide who is invested in your results. Who requires a report? What is their primary focus regarding this program? What information do they want? Who else needs a report? What is their main concern? What information would interest them? Who else is interested in how the program is doing? Besides the stakeholders just listed, are there individuals or groups who might become involved if they had this information? Think about new users, new volunteers, and new funders.

Next, consider which information channels are best to reach the groups you have identified. Some options are articles in the local print and nonprint media, presentations to government bodies such as a city council, a display or presentation at public community events, bookmarks or brochures distributed in the library, and information in the library's newsletter, annual report, and on the library website. If you are not sure—let's say you have a new community partner—ask them how they prefer to get the outcome information. Use Workform 13, Communicate Your Results, to record your ideas.

Now you are ready to write a report—or a press release, brochure, PowerPoint presentation, public service announcement, and so on—for each group you have identified. Your funder probably requires a specific length and format, the library director wants a few talking points, and the Friends group may want a fact sheet to insert in its newsletter. Perhaps the easiest way is to write the longest, most detailed report first, and then borrow from it to create the other items.

In your report, be sure to give context to your findings by describing the program and the need it addresses, as well as the characteristics of your participant group. Report your selected outcomes and indicators (and targets if any) with a short explanation of how they were selected. Describe which (and how many) participants were studied, and then tell how you measured the indicators, attaching any data collection instruments.

At this point you can present the findings of your data analysis, illustrated with graphics. For example, pie charts are good for showing proportions, bar charts are good for comparing numbers or percentages, contingency tables show cross-tabulations, and line charts are good for showing changes or trends over time. Most libraries have the software and staff skills to produce such graphics in-house, but if you do not have the resources, you probably can find graphic design students at the local college. Another possibility is a corporate contribution from the public relations department of a local business.

Tell stories and use quotes to bring the findings to life. Of course, quotes and anecdotes must be chosen carefully. Select ones that are either typical of your users or highlight a program's success. Readers may quote these stories to others, so be sure that they are points worth making.

If you had targets, compare your results to the targets and state whether or not you met them. Yes or no: what does this imply about your program's success? It is essential that you share some of the best thinking from the interpretation meeting and tell who was involved in the interpretation of results and how you reached your conclusions. This will help the readers understand why you met some targets and not others, and why you had some unexpectedly good (or bad) results. These may be factors over which the library has no control, but reporting them is important to aid awareness. If the factors are library- or program-related, that too should be reported, along with the steps you will take to correct the situation. Similarly, you should address any challenges that arose during the data collection and analysis.

Before you distribute your first report—and begin tailoring it for other audiences and uses—give it a trial run by sending it to the people involved in the interpretation and to people who have not seen the data before. Select just a few staff, volunteers, and board members to review the report and to answer a few questions. Does it read easily and clearly? Do the results and their interpretation seem reasonable? What questions do the results raise that are not answered in the report? Would more examples, anecdotes, tables, or charts be helpful?

Now it's time to write the next pieces. Be sure to use language your intended audience will understand and to use their buzzwords (rather than library jargon). Include examples and anecdotes that will appeal to this particular group of people and select the visuals that emphasize the points relevant to this specific audience.

Step 6.3
Use Your Results to Move Forward

The results of your outcome measurement can lead to improvements in a number of areas: program activities, outcome measures and indicators, data collection and analysis, and accountability. They can also be used to

- recruit skilled volunteers and staff
- justify resource (re)allocation
- support budget requests
- plan continuing education
- modify service strategies
- attract potential participants and collaborators
- focus fund-raising
- support long-range planning

The discussion of outcome information can also lead to a problem-solving exchange focused on other issues; for example, identifying training needs among the staff, or identifying a program component that could be altered to improve user outcomes. Perhaps policies, such as criteria for program participation, may be considered for modification.

Program staff should meet regularly to brainstorm, and then implement, changes. For example, your findings might point to a schedule or a location that yields a higher proportion of users achieving an outcome. These effective strategies should be built into the next cycle of the program. It may be that you want to rethink the outcome itself, or the indicators, and your findings will guide that discussion. Of course, your results also provide baseline data to help set realistic target levels for the future.

Once you have initiated program modifications, a segment of your regularly scheduled staff meeting should be put aside to check on how the new aspects of the program are working and to identify any problems. Reports to library decision-makers on the status of the changes will increase your accountability, as well as making the case for additional or different resources and setting the grounds for the next outcome measurement cycle.

Consider improvements to your data collection and analysis process as well. Talk to the individuals who coded, entered, tabulated, and analyzed your data for suggestions on improving instruments, procedures, and timelines. Perhaps do follow-up telephone interviews with a sample of users, or hold a focus group, to discuss modifications that will increase your survey response rate or improve any part of the process that did not work as well as you had anticipated.

Outcome information demonstrates your user-orientation and your emphasis on results and accountability. The effectiveness of your program can be used in publicity to enhance your library's public image, recruit staff and volunteers, and attract potential participants, donors, referral sources, and collaborating agencies and organizations. Consider these and other options in Workform 14, Use Your Results to Move Forward.

To be sure that your outcome information is used, the defining concept of outcomes—that benefit for the end user is the purpose of your program—must be integrated into every aspect of your service, from planning to staff training to decision-making. As your outcome findings aid you in improving your programs, you also improve the chances that your users achieve their outcomes. And then you measure again.

Key Points

Interpretation of your findings gives meaning to your numbers.

Though data analysis can never prove what caused the outcomes, by comparing your findings with those from a different time and by comparing the results of subgroups of participants, you can reach some conclusions to guide your next program cycle.

Reporting results and using results are not the same thing.

Communicate your findings to stakeholders and others depending on what they want to know and how they want to receive the information.

Use the findings to improve your program and your outcome measurement system.

Use the findings for publicity, to recruit and train staff and volunteers, for fund-raising, and for resource allocation—or reallocation.

Notes

1. Morley and others, *A Look at Outcome Measurement*, vii.
2. Harry Hatry and others, *How and Why Nonprofits Use Outcome Information: Findings from a Symposium June 2002* (Washington, DC: Urban Institute, 2003), 11.
3. Harry P. Hatry, Jake Cowan, and Michael Hendricks, *Analyzing Outcome Information: Getting the Most from Data* (Washington, DC: Urban Institute, 2004), 25.

Tool Kit A

Sample Candidate Outcomes

Outcomes must be selected based on your users' needs and the local context. However, many outcomes are equally relevant to different programs. As noted in *How Libraries and Librarians Help,* outcomes are always "specific to a program but not necessarily unique to it."[1]

The purpose of this list is to present ideas and to show the breadth of outcomes used by libraries and other agencies. These examples have been culled from many books, articles, and websites, most of which are listed in the bibliography, as well as from interviews with practitioners. The list is not meant to be comprehensive but suggestive.

If you use a candidate outcome from this list, you must verify its appropriateness for your situation and identify indicators specific to your program. Keep in mind that the outcomes listed here may be either interim or long-range, depending on the characteristics of your program, participants, and context.

Adults will

identify an organization or agency for assistance

contact an organization or agency for assistance

make informed retirement decisions

make informed investment decisions

make informed health-care decisions

make informed consumer decisions

make informed legal decisions

make career changes

develop job-related skills

determine career possibilities

start a business

determine the education necessary for a career change

improve their job level

find a job

home-school their children

solve a business- or work-related problem

make an informed decision regarding their business

make an informed decision regarding an organization

learn about a social or political issue

learn more about a hobby or a topic of personal interest

increase a personal skill

learn how to use new technology

learn how to use genealogical (or any other topic-specific) databases

make progress researching family history

reunite with a "lost" family member

learn about family medical history

learn about own cultural heritage

learn about others' cultural heritage

increase community involvement

participate in a public meeting

participate in a community activity

represent self in court

develop tolerance for others

pass the GED exam

pass the SAT exam

pass the naturalization exam

pass a job-related exam

become a citizen

be promoted at work

expand worldview through cross-cultural experiences

engage in global dialogue

increase tolerance for others

broaden a social network

gain mental sustenance

enhance academic performance

enhance work performance

improve interpersonal skills

improve interpersonal relationships

improve problem-solving skills

solve a personal problem

research a health issue

become more employable

experience life enrichment

enjoy a sense of escape from daily life

sustain a sense of identity

apply and value own education (volunteers)

increase sense of responsibility to others (volunteers)

increase intergenerational understanding

be able to parent appropriately, successfully

feel emotionally supported

enhance personal well-being

enhance emotional well-being

enhance material well-being

improve personal development (e.g., good self-image)

improve self-determination (e.g., sense of personal control)

improve self-sufficiency (e.g., sense of independence)

enjoy enhanced social inclusion

enjoy social involvement

improve physical health

make healthy lifestyle choices

improve legal status

improve role status

enjoy increased family involvement

make an informed decision regarding housing

improve living or residential status

improve physical health

make an informed decision regarding education

become a student

complete school or college

feel part of the community

find new direction

acquire new skills (in a specific area)

get emotional support or confirmation

increase pleasure or happiness

feel more relaxed

increase sense of personal efficacy (i.e., ability to make things happen)

change outlook on life and future prospects

make progress toward a goal

decrease transaction "costs" for information (e.g., time, money, energy, convenience) adapt to life in a new country and culture (for new immigrants)

bridge cultural landscapes (immigrants)

preserve native culture

enhance decision-making skills

make a personal decision

change self-perception (e.g., self-esteem and self-confidence)

improve quality of family life

create ideas or objects

increase communication skills

gain heightened awareness of community

learn about local transportation

gain ability to move independently around the community on local transportation

increase creative self-expression

experience a shift in peer attitudes and respect

have an opportunity to participate in public discourse

receive appropriate and meaningful referral to community services

participate in the democratic process

improve personal finances

prepare annual tax return

gain technology skills

gain research skills

make informed decision about travel

take a trip

know how to evaluate information found on the Web

have a greater interest in local history (or any particular topic)

have increased access to library resources

have greater understanding of library policies and procedures

learn about a favorite author

foster a love of reading in his or her children (adult new learner)

read to his or her children (adult new learner)

read the Bible or other religious text (adult new learner)

read the newspaper or a magazine (adult new learner)

comprehend more of what is read (adult new learner)

use reading skills in daily life (adult new learner)

read for pleasure

become motivated (to learn or do something)

see themselves as capable (of learning or doing something)

change their attitude (about a particular topic)

In addition to the outcomes above, Older Adults will

sustain a sense of identity

sustain a sense of dignity

contribute to local history project

increase social interaction

experience reduced sense of isolation

expand a social network

share memories and experiences

have thought processes stimulated

focus on healthier times

enhance personal well-being

broaden a social network

continue to live safely at home

learn to grandparent appropriately

function independently

improve living or residential status

share life wisdom

make independent choices

practice life review

create a memoir for younger family members

feel connected to larger world

Children and Young Adults will

stimulate their imagination

increase their attention span

develop social skills

experience an alternative world (through fantasy)

develop tolerance for others

increase trust of adults

increase self-confidence

make independent choices

increase multicultural understanding

increase intergenerational understanding

enjoy vicarious experiences

be able to survive as "latchkey kids"

translate and read in English for their parents (children of non-English speakers)

make new friendships (outside of classroom)

increase their vocabulary

improve their school grades

improve their verbal skills

have less idle time after school

have less opportunity for illegal and unhealthy activities

improve interpersonal skills

show increased interest in school

improve school attendance rate

complete school

enter college

improve critical thinking or problem-solving skills

improve academic test scores

decrease involvement in gang and illegal activity

decrease incidence of substance abuse and other unhealthy activities

expand the diversity of their friendships

have an adult role model

know where to go to access help

enjoy something good to do or somewhere good to go after school

increase career goals and life expectations

have an adult to talk to

will be safe from danger or harm

feel emotionally supported

increase self-esteem

gain technology skills

gain research skills

make informed decisions

know how to evaluate information found on the Web

participate in the democratic process

make informed consumer decisions

make informed health-care decisions

increase communication skills

have heightened awareness of community

increase creative self-expression

learn to work collaboratively

develop new ability to interact with strangers, adults

increase sense of responsibility

improve problem-solving skills

improve decision-making skills

have a greater interest in a particular topic

have increased access to library resources

have greater understanding of library policies and procedures

develop a love of reading

learn about a favorite author

increase sense of personal efficacy (ability to make things happen)

create ideas or objects

NOTE

1. Joan Durrance and Karen E. Fisher, *How Libraries and Librarians Help: A Guide to Identifying User-Centered Outcomes* (Chicago: American Library Association, 2004), 66.

Tool Kit B

Measuring Staff Training Outcomes

Outcome measurement is a user-centered approach to the assessment of services that are based on user needs and designed to achieve change for the user. In other words, *outcome measurement assesses the impact—defined as change in knowledge, skills, attitude, behavior, or condition of the end user—of a service or program.*

Training is, by definition, an outcome-based activity, since the goal is always impact on the trainees; the purpose is to stimulate or contribute to a change. When we train library staff, our intent is to facilitate them in

- learning something new (change in knowledge)
- altering an attitude (change in attitude)
- improving how they do something (change in skill or behavior)
- reaching a personal or agency goal (change in behavior or status)

So it logically follows that training evaluations should assess change in the learner. Yet evaluations of staff training rarely do this. Instead, workshop evaluations usually tell us the satisfaction level of participants and, more specifically, what they liked and didn't like. This is because the typical workshop evaluation is a survey with questions that focus only on training inputs such as the presenter, facility, handouts, and refreshments. For example, "Please rate the presenter's knowledge of the subject." "Did the handouts enhance the presentation?" Gathering such *reactions* or *satisfaction ratings* is necessary to help us improve the appeal and quality of future training. Trainers know that favorable reactions to training will not guarantee learning, but unfavorable reactions usually undermine learning. See figures B-1, B-2, and B-3 for sample reaction/satisfaction surveys.

Measuring outcomes—the actual effect of training on participants—is also essential. No matter how popular a certain trainer or how well received a workshop, if the training does not result in the desired impact it is unsuccessful. So the basic question both when planning and evaluating training must be: *what impact does the library expect the training to have on the participants?*

Workshop Satisfaction Survey

1. Please rate the *workshop content* by indicating your agreement with the following statements. Please circle your answer:

	Strongly Disagree	Disagree	Agree	Strongly Agree
a. Interesting	1	2	3	4
b. Well organized	1	2	3	4
c. Met my expectations	1	2	3	4
d. Fit my level of experience	1	2	3	4
e. Included sufficient examples	1	2	3	4
f. Expanded my thinking	1	2	3	4
g. Relevant to my work	1	2	3	4

Other comments:

2. Please rate the *presenter*:

	Strongly Disagree	Disagree	Agree	Strongly Agree
a. Well informed	1	2	3	4
b. Well prepared	1	2	3	4
c. Easy to understand	1	2	3	4
d. Stimulated learning	1	2	3	4
e. Involved participants	1	2	3	4
f. Sensitive to dynamics	1	2	3	4
g. Relevant examples	1	2	3	4
h. Answered questions well	1	2	3	4

Other comments:

3. Please rate the *workbook*:

	Strongly Disagree	Disagree	Agree	Strongly Agree
a. Not useful at all	1	2	3	4
b. Helpful during the session	1	2	3	4
c. Useful for future reference	1	2	3	4
d. Clearly written	1	2	3	4
e. Valuable information	1	2	3	4
f. Well organized	1	2	3	4

Other comments:

4. Please rate the *logistics*:

	Strongly Disagree	Disagree	Agree	Strongly Agree
a. Easy registration	1	2	3	4
b. Convenient day or date	1	2	3	4
c. Convenient time	1	2	3	4
d. Convenient location	1	2	3	4
e. Comfortable room	1	2	3	4
f. Good acoustics	1	2	3	4
g. Sufficient breaks	1	2	3	4
h. Reasonable fee	1	2	3	4

Other comments:

5. I would recommend this workshop to others. ___Yes ___ No

If not, why not:

Thank you for completing the survey.

InfoPeople Workshop Evaluation Form

Workshop Name:_____   Date: _____

1. Overall, I found the workshop:

    Poor   1   2   3   4   5   6   7   8   9   10   *Excellent*

2. The pace of the workshop was: ___ Too slow   ___ Too fast   ___ Just right

3. Today I learned: ___ More than I expected   ___ As much as I could absorb

    ___ About what I expected   ___ A little bit

4. Please rate the workshop instructor(s) in the following areas (circle a number)

    a. Knowledge of the subject matter:

        Poor   1   2   3   4   5   6   7   8   9   10   *Excellent*

    b. Presentation style:

        Poor   1   2   3   4   5   6   7   8   9   10   *Excellent*

    c. Overall effectiveness:

        Poor   1   2   3   4   5   6   7   8   9   10   *Excellent*

5. How helpful were the workshop materials?

    ___ Not helpful at all   ___ Helpful during workshop   ___ Very useful; will use again

6. My type of library:

    ___ Academic   ___ Public   ___ School   ___ Special   ___ Library System   ___ I'm not from a library

    ___ Other: _____

7. What I found *most* valuable was: (e.g., most useful topics, teaching techniques, useful metaphors)

8. What I found *least* valuable was:

9. What I would change about this workshop is:

10. How will you use the skills learned in this course?

11. How did you first hear or learn about this course?

Optional: Name_____   Library/Branch_____

Workshop Benefit Survey

All answers are confidential. In order to link your future answers to these, please give us a four-digit identification number _____ (e.g., birth date, last four digits of phone or social security number).

1. What did you gain from this workshop? (*check all that apply*)

    a. _____ New information I can use immediately

    b. _____ New information I may use in the future

    c. _____ Expanded understanding of things I already know

    d. _____ New techniques or behaviors I can use immediately

    e. _____ New techniques or behaviors I may use in the future

    f. _____ Reinforcement of behaviors I already use

    g. _____ Answers to my questions

    h. _____ Resource materials I can use

2. To what extent did the workshop meet your expectations?

Not at all	*A little*	*Mostly*	*Completely*
1	2	3	4

3. To what extent did the workshop make you think?

Not at all	*A little*	*Quite a bit*	*A great deal*
1	2	3	4

4. To what extent did the workshop make you want to learn more on the topic?

Not at all	*A little*	*Quite a bit*	*A great deal*
1	2	3	4

5. To what extent did the workshop motivate you to share this information with coworkers?

Not at all	*A little*	*Quite a bit*	*A great deal*
1	2	3	4

6. How do you plan to use the information and resources from this workshop?

7. What one new technique or behavior do you plan to try?

8. Please describe when and how you will use it.

(*Cont.*)

9. As you think about the next three months, check the answer which best describes the degree to which you will engage in the following practices.

List Behaviors	Almost never	Seldom	Sometimes	Often
a. _____	_____	_____	_____	_____
b. _____	_____	_____	_____	_____
c. _____	_____	_____	_____	_____
d. _____	_____	_____	_____	_____

10. During the workshop, the following actions were suggested. Please mark "yes" for the ones you intend to try.

List Actions	Almost never	Seldom	Sometimes	Often
a. _____	_____	_____	_____	_____
b. _____	_____	_____	_____	_____
c. _____	_____	_____	_____	_____
d. _____	_____	_____	_____	_____

Thank you for completing the survey.

Before discussing how the impact or outcomes of training can be evaluated, we must back up a minute and reconsider the definition of *outcome measurement*, which refers to the impact on the end user of a service. If library staff are trained, are the trainees considered the end users? Or is staff training a vehicle for providing a new or improved service to the library customers, the end users of libraries?

In outcome measurement terms, staff training is usually considered an intermediate outcome, that is, the first in a series of results that will ultimately provide impact on the library user. (Those later impacts are then called outcomes or long-range outcomes.) In some projects, though, staff members are designated as the end users of a training program.

Outcome measurement requires that the desired outcomes are determined during the initial planning of a service (in this case, training). We know that most training impacts are at the learning, skills, or behavior levels. *Specifying exactly what learning, skills, or behavior changes a workshop will elicit forces trainers and administrators to make their assumptions explicit and clarifies what the training activities should be.* In this vein, some trainers develop learning objectives for their workshops; these define the desired impact by stating exactly what the participants will be able to do after a given training session or series and what evidence of accomplishment (or indicator) is expected.

For example, some learning objectives for a management training course might be: "At the end of this course, participants will be able to identify five common leadership styles, explain the importance of effective communication in motivating employees, develop a strategy for team-building, and describe three effective conflict-resolution techniques."

In outcome measurement terms, the four activities listed in the objectives (identify, explain, develop, describe) are indicators of intermediate outcomes; they identify what we can expect to see that lets us know that participants have experienced changes (in this case, in knowledge).

Tips on Measuring Reaction or Satisfaction

- Typical areas to ask participants their opinions about the training include the relevance of training content; difficulty or ease of course material; ability and style of instructor; course design and schedule; class size; and facility comfort.
- Note that trainees' satisfaction with training is directly related to their willingness to attend. Participants who attend involuntarily are rarely happy. Often they are aware that the requirement to attend means that a supervisor is dissatisfied with their knowledge or behavior. The evaluation form can ask a question that allows you to identify the responses of unwilling participants. For instance, "Was it your choice to attend this workshop?" Some evaluators tabulate and analyze such responses separately from those of voluntary participants.
- Only ask what you really need to know. For example, if you are using a new facility, you will want to ask about it. However, if it is a facility that has been consistently excellent and popular, you need not ask about it.
- Keep the directions and format simple. This is an evaluation form, not a test of a person's ability to follow complex directions.
- Number each question for ease of data analysis and reporting.
- Require all participants to complete the evaluation form before leaving. Take-home forms usually do not return, and those that do are skewed. Depending on the personalities of the trainees, you may receive only negative responses, or only positive ones. Similarly, *voluntary* evaluation forms are usually filled out by people at the two ends of the satisfaction spectrum.
- Allow enough time for evaluations to be completed thoughtfully.
- Consider providing incentives for participating in the evaluation.
- If the training includes several sessions, consider doing an evaluation after the first session as well as at the end of the series. The information gained from the first session can be used to improve the next sessions.
- The survey should be anonymous so that trainees feel free to give frank responses. You are not interested in the opinions of any one person; instead, you will tabulate and analyze the results to see what the majority of trainees (or the majority of trainees in one job classification, or the majority of trainees in one department) feel.
- If you offer a rating scale, avoid the usual three choices of "unsatisfactory," "satisfactory," and "excellent." It has been shown that most participants will select the middle of three choices most of the time. If 99 percent of trainees select "satisfactory" for all five of your questions, you do not find out much useful information. Instead, offer four choices such as "poor," "satisfactory," "good," and "excellent."
- It is best to use some of each of the two kinds of questions: "supply" and "select." *Supply questions* include no answer categories. The respondent must create an answer. These can be short-answer questions or longer essay questions. The questions can be

closed-ended or open-ended. If you think a yes or no is sufficient, use a select question instead. Save supply questions for situations where you want descriptions or explanations from respondents. For example, you might ask a very open-ended question such as "Please describe. . . ." *Select questions* provide a limited range of responses; for example, yes-no questions, ratings or rankings, checklists, and multiple-choice questions. Select questions leave you in control of the answers, which makes the analysis easy. But they do not allow for respondents to add descriptive or explanatory comments. Another approach is to ask only some questions as yes-no. For example, "Was the trainer well prepared? Yes or No." You can ask for elaboration on negative responses with "If no, please explain."

- A question such as, "If this workshop is offered again, what would you change?" often yields the most useful information. Some evaluators, though, avoid this and other open-ended questions because it is difficult to tabulate and analyze the responses.
- Other problems with open-ended questions are that they take more time for the participant to answer, many participants will just leave a blank, and some answers will not be clear or complete.
- Allow space for "Other comments." Although this is where you will hear mundane complaints (e.g., the coffee was weak), you may also get answers to questions you had not thought to ask. For example, a trainee might write, "Please schedule more training on Tuesdays." Upon investigation there may be scheduling issues you were unaware of.

Learning Outcomes

If learning is the intended outcome, the evaluation should center on the basic question, *"Did the trainee learn the material?"* In some cases, participants can demonstrate a skill to the instructor before leaving the premises; for example, find a designated piece of information in a database. Or the participants can answer a quiz on their newly acquired knowledge; for example, list three sources of prices for vintage Hummel figures.

The most common form of evaluation, though, is the survey that asks participants about their comfort level with the new skill or about their intent to use it. For example, participants may say they feel more comfortable about their ability to serve people with hearing loss after a disability awareness workshop. Or they may say that they intend to practice their basic Spanish vocabulary after a Survival Spanish workshop.

Note that learning outcomes may not only be the acquisition of new information or techniques. Trainees may also gain expanded understanding; refocused attention; application of information in a new context; help in explaining something to others; reinforcement of an idea; or commitment to action (intent to change behavior).

Learning may be the only result of training that is evaluated. Usually it is the trainer or administrator who is most interested in this type of evaluation, because it checks whether the instructional methods are effective. Sometimes, though, a change in performance quality is the intended outcome of training. In that case, learning is considered an intermediate outcome, necessary to achieve the long-range outcome of behavior change. The central question then is, *"Did the trainee change his or her behavior on the job because of the knowledge gain?"* To answer this question, you may need to assess on-the-job performance to see if training made a difference. See figures B-4, B-5, and B-6 for sample surveys that measure learning outcomes.

Planning for Library Services for People with Disabilities

California State Library Workshop #3 Post-Survey

Your four-digit identification number: _____

Directions: For each question, please circle the number that you feel best describes your opinion. On the number scale, 1 means "I disagree strongly," 2 means "I disagree," 3 means "I agree," and 4 means "I agree strongly." If no number scale is given, please write a very brief response.

1. I am considerably more knowledgeable now than I was last week about *community collaboration*.

   1 2 3 4

2. I can explain to colleagues these two new ideas on the why and how of *community collaboration*:

   1.

   2.

3. I am considerably more knowledgeable now than I was last week about *grantsmanship*.

   1 2 3 4

4. I can list at least two possible grant sources to consider when planning the continuation of our program.

   1.

   2.

5. I am considerably more knowledgeable now than I was last week about *volunteerism*.

   1 2 3 4

6. I can share with colleagues these two new ideas about recruiting and using volunteers:

   1.

   2.

7. I am considerably more knowledgeable now than I was before on *outcome measurement*.

   1 2 3 4

8. I am confident that I can complete an outcome measurement plan for evaluating our project.

   1 2 3 4

   If not, please explain:

9. I am confident that I can complete the LSTA application by the deadline.

   1 2 3 4

   If not, please explain:

Thank you for answering this survey frankly and completely.

LAMA Institute on Outcome Measurement

Post-Workshop Survey

Your four-digit identification number: _____

1   How do you rate your current overall knowledge of outcome measurement?

      Excellent   Good   Novice

2. How do you rate your ability to explain the differences between traditional evaluation and outcome measurement to a colleague?

      High   Moderate   Low

3. How do you rate your ability to differentiate between library programs and services that are suitable for outcome measurement and those that are not?

      High   Moderate   Low

4. How do you rate your confidence level in planning and implementing outcome measurement for a selected new program or service?

      High   Moderate   Low

5. What new idea or piece of information will you put to use immediately?

Thank you for completing the survey.

Follow-Up to Workshop Benefit Survey [Send out one month after workshop]

Your four-digit identification number: _____

1. Have you learned more about (subject of workshop) since the workshop?   ___Yes   ___No

   If no, please specify what obstacles kept you from doing so:

   If yes, please specify how you found more information on the topic and how you used it:

2. Have you shared the workshop information with your coworkers?   ___Yes   ___No

   If no, please specify what obstacles kept you from doing so:

   If yes, please specify when and how you did this:

3. At the close of the workshop, you specified a new technique or behavior you meant to try. What was it?

4. Did you try the new technique or behavior?   ___Yes   ___No

   If no, please specify what obstacles kept you from doing so:

   If yes, please specify when and in what situation you used it:

Was your use of the new technique or behavior successful? Please describe.

(Cont.)

5. As you think about the past three months, check the answer which best describes the degree to which you will engage in the following practices.

List Behaviors	Almost never	Seldom	Sometimes	Often
a. _____	_____	_____	_____	_____
b. _____	_____	_____	_____	_____
c. _____	_____	_____	_____	_____
d. _____	_____	_____	_____	_____

6. During the workshop, the following actions were suggested. Please mark "yes" for the ones you have tried.

List Actions	Yes	No
a. _____	_____	_____
b. _____	_____	_____
c. _____	_____	_____
d. _____	_____	_____

Thank you for completing the survey.

Tips on Measuring Learning Outcomes

- Develop the evaluation instruments as you develop the training objectives and content. This is less work for the trainer and ensures that the questions relate directly to what is taught.
- As with workshop satisfaction surveys, responses are anonymous. Again, your interest as an evaluator is not in any one individual's learning, but in the effect of training on all the participants. Results will be aggregated and reported as one group, for example, "100 trainees felt . . ."
- Again, it is essential that all trainees complete the evaluation before they leave the training session.
- The use of pre- and posttests is most common because you need a baseline from which to measure gains in knowledge. Usually, pre- and posttests take the form of surveys. Typically, the pretest survey is administered at the beginning of the workshop, though some trainers prefer to send it out ahead of time so they can see the participants' self-ratings as the trainers fine-tune the workshop activities.
- Surveys are the most common evaluation instrument, but keep in mind that asking participants about their knowledge or skill level does not really assess that; instead, surveys measure what the participants perceive to be true. Also, results are often skewed because participants know they are "supposed to say" that they know more after the training than they did before it.
- A more reliable type of pre- and posttest is a paper and pencil quiz on the subject. This may have multiple-choice questions (e.g., "Select the situation in which you should ask a colleague to assist a customer in your place"); true-false questions (e.g., "If you see a patron whom you do not like approach the desk, ask a colleague to take your place"); short-answer questions (e.g., "List below three public situations in which the police

should be called"); and fill-in-the-blank questions (e.g., "You should greet each customer by saying _____"). A combination of question types is best. Again, the test is given before and after training. One or more subject specialists should work with the training evaluator to design the questions.

- Whether using a survey or a quiz, usually the same questions are asked in the pre-and posttests, but the order of the questions might be different to ensure that the participants must look closely at each question.

- Performance tests can be used instead of paper and pencil tests. Performance tests are especially useful for technical or manual skills or for skills that we can see. For example, at the end of a training session, participants might be asked to demonstrate the correct procedures for coding an HTML document for a web page. Youth services trainees might be asked to give a brief puppet show demonstration. Customer service trainees may be asked to role-play a specific situation.

- When using a pre-and posttest design, it is important that you are able to match the responses to the pretest with those to the posttest. Yet you want people to remain anonymous. The easiest way to handle this dilemma is to ask each respondent to put an ID number on the form; only they know the meaning of the numbers, but you can use them to match the forms. For instance, people might use the last four digits of their social security number, phone number, or license plate. Similarly, if a performance test is used, the observer or instructor uses only the ID code on the forms.

- If it is clear that the participants have no knowledge of the subject of the training, then a pretest (survey or quiz) is not needed. For example, if you are training staff to use a new automated system, you can assume that any knowledge the participants have at the end of the training has been learned in the class.

- Some evaluators use a variation of the classic pre- and posttest survey so that participants only fill out the survey once, after the training. In this approach, the form gives an instruction such as, "Please indicate your knowledge or skill level for each topic prior to the training program. Then indicate your present knowledge or skill level in the second column." For each topic (e.g., the legality of personal questions during a job interview) the respondent would select "very poor," "poor," "medium," or "high" under the heading "Prior" and then again under the heading "Present." This type of survey has the same perception problem as standard pre- and posttest surveys.

- All survey forms and tests must be pilot-tested before use with actual trainees. Ask colleagues or people from another course to use them to be sure that the directions are clear and that the questions elicit the information you need.

- Interviews can also be used to assess knowledge gain, but they are more time-intensive and therefore more costly than surveys. Sometimes interviewing a sample of trainees can clarify unexpected or unclear survey results.

- Learning evaluations accurately measure the amount of knowledge acquired at the time of the test or survey. Remember that in no way do learning evaluations indicate long-term knowledge gain or skill retention. Nor do they indicate that actual on-the-job behavior will be affected.

- When asking about intent, it is a good idea to do a follow-up. Sending out a short survey (even one question on a postcard) will give you additional information at the same time that it serves as a reminder and reinforcement for the participant.

Behavior Outcomes

Changes in behavior and on-the-job performance quality, though not often assessed, are usually the real goals of training. For example, library staff need to feel comfortable serving people with disabilities or be able to communicate with Spanish-speaking people for a specific reason: so that service to customers is improved. It is not enough for participants to demonstrate the selected intermediate outcomes on a quiz or survey if they do not change their actual behavior with customers. *The long-range outcomes of training should always be changes in behavior or condition.*

In other words, a librarian who improves her reference skills should be able to perform her job better. Indicators of this might be the ability to answer more questions accurately or to answer more questions at the point of first contact without referring them on. A library employee who improves his customer service skills should also be able to perform his job better. Indicators of this might be a decrease in customer complaints that require management intervention, or an increase in customer satisfaction levels on an annual survey.

In order to measure long-range training outcomes, trainees must be assessed weeks or months after the workshop itself. Participants must have a chance to transfer their training to the workplace and exhibit their mastery of new skills or behaviors on the job. To see if the new behaviors are retained, another time gap must occur. Such longitudinal assessments are more difficult to implement than immediate assessments, and the results are more difficult to analyze because the passage of time has allowed more factors to intervene, muddying the waters of what is attributable to training.

Tips on Measuring Change in Behavior or Performance

- Keep in mind that behavior change is based on many factors. Training programs can be successful in knowledge and skill transfer, yet not result in changed behavior on the job. Participants may choose not to change their behavior due to various reasons, including lack of management support for new behavior; lack of collegial support for change; and lack of sufficient rewards to motivate change.
- The most common approaches to assessing behavior change are observation (by a trained observer) of the employee on the job; observation (by a trained observer) of the employee in a simulation (e.g., fire drill); standardized skills testing; employee self-report (on a workshop follow-up form); interviews with others (such as customers, coworkers, or supervisors); and interviews with the employee. These are listed from most direct to least direct; the more direct the better, because otherwise your results may confuse actual change with perception of change.
- Of course, some performance outcomes, such as decision-making skills, are not directly observable. Indicators of these skills must be identified and assessed instead. How will a staff member's decision-making skill manifest itself on the job?
- Data on behavioral change is most reliable when more than one source of information is used. You might interview the trainee and the supervisor, for example.
- One challenge with assessment on the job is that anonymity is lost and individuals are being observed as individuals. The evaluation results, therefore, could be used to blame

or punish individuals rather than to document how training impacts work and to improve the training processes as necessary. This is an extremely important and sensitive issue. In a situation where training and performance are linked by the administration as a method to reach institutional goals, this must be explained clearly by the administration to the trainees. Otherwise, an outside evaluator who does not know the participants should do the assessment and report only aggregated information, using no names or identifying information. If this approach is taken, it too must be explained clearly to all.

- Knowing that they are being observed can make people uncomfortable and affect the behavior that is being watched. Therefore it is necessary to observe any one behavior more than once.
- Another concern with observation is that the report can be subjective; it is essential to have an objective, trained observer.
- Depending on how much the trainee needs to know, how difficult the tasks are, how frequently the tasks are used on the job, and how critical the nature of the tasks is, a trainee may demonstrate behavior change immediately or not. Because people need time to practice new behavior before they feel competent at it and use it regularly, behavior change is usually not assessed until a few months after completion of training.
- When selecting the right time to assess behavior change, take into account how often the new skill is used on the job. For example, if it is used multiple times each day, it can be assessed sooner than if it is a weekly task. Also keep in mind the cycles of your data collection method. If supervisory reports are submitted monthly, and you want to use them as part of the evaluation, you will have to schedule your assessment accordingly.
- Some evaluators repeat the assessment six or even nine months after the training to see if the new behavior persists.
- Social scientists debate whether attitude precedes behavior or vice versa. It has been shown that when a person's attitude changes, his or her behavior will be affected. But it has also been proved that when a person is forced to change his or her behavior, the relevant attitudes will be affected. For instance, if a person has negative attitudes toward people from other countries and shows negative behavior toward such people, forcing him to change either behavior (e.g., sharing a work space) or attitude (e.g., witnessing that respected friends have positive attitudes toward foreigners) can affect the other. In some soft skills training, such as customer service, attitudes and behaviors interplay, so the evaluation should cover both aspects.
- One difficulty with the delayed nature of behavior change assessment is logistical—finding the trainee and gaining their (and their supervisors') cooperation. Some trainers prepare for this by asking both people to sign a learning contract before the training. Others send periodic reminders to keep trainees aware that they will be assessed.
- Another concern with delayed evaluation is that the passage of time allows other factors to intercede so that the assessment may not really measure the effects of training per se. For example, the staff member may show no improvement in reference skills because her job responsibilities have changed. Or conversely, she may indeed show an increase in the percentage of reference questions answered within a half hour because the library has licensed new electronic databases.
- Whether evaluation is immediate or delayed, training can never take all of the credit or all of the blame for behavior change. This is okay; evaluation of training is not supposed to be rocket science. However, if you want to greatly increase the chances that

results actually derive from training, you must use a control group of employees who have not received the training but are similarly assessed. Of course, this presents logistical as well as ethical problems and is not recommended.

SOURCES

Fink, Arlene, and others. *How to Ask Survey Questions*. Thousand Oaks, CA: Sage, 2002.

————. *The Survey Handbook*. Thousand Oaks, CA: Sage, 2002.

Gill, Stephen J. *Linking Training to Performance Goals.* Info-Line issue no. 9606. Alexandria, VA: American Society for Training and Development, 1996.

Hacker, Deborah Grafinger. *Testing for Learning Outcomes*. Revised edition. Info-Line issue no. 8907. Alexandria, VA: American Society for Training and Development, 1998.

Merwin, Sandra. *Evaluation: Ten Significant Ways for Measuring and Improving Training Impact*. Wiley, 1999.

O'Neill, Mary. *How to Focus a Training Evaluation*. Info-Line issue no. 9605. Alexandria, VA: American Society for Training and Development, 1996.

Robinson, Dana Gaines, and James C. Robinson. *Training for Impact*. Jossey-Bass, 1989.

Taylor-Powell, Ellen. *Questionnaire Design: Asking Questions with a Purpose*. Program Development and Evaluation, University of Wisconsin-Extension, 2000.

Taylor-Powell, Ellen, and Marcus Renner. *Collecting Evaluation Data: End-of-Session Questionnaires*. Program Development and Evaluation, University of Wisconsin-Extension, 2000.

Waagen, Alice K. *Essentials for Evaluation*. Info-Line issue no. 9705. Alexandria, VA: American Society for Training and Development, 1997.

Tool Kit C

Sample Confidentiality Forms

Sample Confidentiality Statement

The appropriate statement is to be provided with all written surveys, and read aloud preceding all interviews, during the course of the outcome measurement study.

For anonymous responses:

We need your help to improve our program. We are not asking for your name or any other identifying information on this form. All of your answers to these questions are recorded anonymously. No one will know who answered which questions in what way. Your responses will be recorded along with many others, and only a summary of the total results will be shared with others. Although we are asking about your experiences, we are looking for patterns of experience among all the users of/participants in _____.

For confidential responses:

We need your help to improve our program. All of your answers to these questions will be kept confidential. We are asking for your name/identification number only so that we can compare your answers now to your answers in the future. After that, your name/identification number will be removed from this form. Your responses will be recorded along with many others, and only a summary of the total results will be shared with others. Although we are asking about your experiences, we are looking for patterns of experience among all the users of/participants in _____.

Sample Pledge of Confidentiality for Data Collectors

I understand that:

> I may be collecting information of a personal and sensitive nature.
>
> Individuals participating in this study have been assured that their names will not be disclosed and that all information will be kept confidential. The responsibility of fulfilling this assurance of confidentiality begins with me.

In recognition of this responsibility, I hereby give my personal pledge to:

> Keep confidential the names of all respondents, all information and opinions collected during the data collection process, and any information learned incidentally while collecting the data.
>
> Refrain from discussing or disclosing, except privately with my data collection supervisor, information that may in any way identify or be linked to a particular individual.
>
> Terminate data collection immediately if I encounter a respondent or begin reviewing a record for an individual whom I know personally, and contact my supervisor for further instructions.
>
> Take precautions to prevent access by others to data in my possession.
>
> Take all other actions within my power to safeguard the privacy of respondents and protect the confidentiality of information I collect.
>
> Devote my best efforts to ensure that there is compliance with the required procedures by persons I supervise.

Signed: _____

Date: _____

Source: Sample Pledge of Confidentiality for Data Collectors reprinted from *Measuring Program Outcomes: A Practical Approach* (Alexandria, VA: United Way of America, 1996). Used by permission, United Way of America.

Tool Kit D

Tips on Developing Questionnaires

Types of Questions

There are two basic types of questions: open-ended and closed-ended. The best questionnaires are a combination of the two types of questions.

Closed-Ended Questions

Closed-ended questions give the respondent alternative answers to choose among. Examples include yes-no, true-false, ratings, rankings, checklists, scales, and multiple-choice questions.

The advantage to closed-ended questions for the respondent is that they are easy and fast to answer. The advantage to you is that—because you have kept control over the possible answers—they are easy to tabulate and analyze. The disadvantages are that the respondent does not have the opportunity to explain, and if you have not listed the correct responses—or all the possibilities—the information you gather may not be meaningful.

Open-Ended Questions

Open-ended questions are sometimes called supply questions because the respondent, not the evaluator, must supply the answers. Examples are short-answer, essay, or fill-in-the-blank questions. Sometimes an open-ended question is used to allow the respondent to elaborate on a closed-ended question; for example, "please describe" or "please explain" or "if not, why?"

The main advantage of open-ended questions is that respondents can express themselves—without you inadvertently limiting answers—and that you hear what they want to say in their own words. The main disadvantages are that open-ended questions take more time for the respondent to answer (tempting people to skip the question) and more time for you to analyze.

Sometimes open-ended questions are used just to discover the range of possible answers, and future versions of the survey use that information in closed-ended questions.

Content

When you are deciding what to ask your participants, discard any questions that ask for unnecessary information or that the participants cannot answer accurately and honestly. To test for these criteria, use Workform 9 with your draft questions.

Wording of Questions

It is essential to write your questions in clear, focused language so that the participant will understand the questions and so that you will be able to code the answers. Make the questions short, eliminating all extra words and any library jargon. Ask "How long did it take you to check out your book?" rather than "Tell us about your experience with circulation."

Strip your questionnaire of any leading questions or biased language. For example, ask "Please rate the usefulness of the new service" rather than "Please list all the ways the new service is more useful for you," which assumes that the service is indeed more useful. Be sure that each question only asks one thing. In other words, avoid a question like, "Was the book fun and easy to read?" which is really two questions. Don't ask negative questions such as, "Answer yes or no: I didn't find the instructions difficult." Don't ask about events or experiences a long time past, and if you must ask about the past, be specific as to the time period in question.

If you use a rating scale, be sure it includes response options from very negative to very positive and that you have the same number of each. Avoid the typical "unsatisfactory," "satisfactory," and "more than satisfactory," because most people will select the middle option most of the time.

If you offer response categories, make them as specific as possible. For example, use "every day" or "once a week" rather than "frequently." Make sure the response categories don't overlap. For example, "Do you read to your child more than once a week or daily?"

If you are surveying a cultural or ethnic group other than your own, be sure to get input as you develop the questionnaire so that you don't accidentally offend anyone. Also pilot-test it with representatives of the user group to be sure that they understand the questions and are willing to answer them.

Order of Questions

Start the questionnaire with short, clear instructions. End it with a thank-you.

The order of the questions should have a logical flow to make it as easy as possible for people to answer them. For example, you might cluster the questions by topic. Ask the least personal—and least intrusive—questions first to ease people into your survey. Be sure that the early questions are easy to answer and directly related to the service or program you are evaluating. More people will answer sensitive and wide-ranging questions once they are into the survey than will answer them up front. Similarly, the wording and order of questions are not as significant in a posttest as in a pretest; users who are familiar with you or your program are usually less distrustful.

A posttest questionnaire should ask the same questions as the pretest, using the same wording. Often, though, evaluators change the order of the questions to ensure that the respondents actually read each question carefully.

Format

Formatting a questionnaire refers to the obvious concerns of font clarity and size, but also to the effect of the layout on a participant's willingness and ability to complete the survey. For example, be sure that the answer options for any question are on the same page as the question itself. Allow enough space for open-ended questions. Keep the response categories or points on a rating scale the same throughout the questionnaire.

Use paper and ink colors that are easy to read, and allow plenty of white space around the questions. These will help the respondent. To help your data processor, number each question sequentially.

SOURCES

Abravanel, Martin D. *Surveying Clients about Outcomes*. Washington, DC: Urban Institute, 2003.

Burroughs, Catherine M., and Fred B. Wood. *Measuring the Difference*. Seattle, WA: National Network of Libraries of Medicine, Pacific Northwest Region, 2000.

Fink, Arlene, and Jacqueline Kosecoff. *How to Ask Survey Questions*. Thousand Oaks, CA: Sage, 2000.

Peterson, Robert A. *Constructing Effective Questionnaires*. Thousand Oaks, CA: Sage, 1999.

Project STAR for the Corporation for National Service. *Beginning with the End in Mind*. May 2004. http://projectstar.org/star/AmeriCorps.pmtoolkit.htm.

Taylor-Powell, Ellen, and others. *Questionnaire Design: Asking Questions with a Purpose*. Madison: University of Wisconsin Extension, 1998.

United Way. *Measuring Program Outcomes: A Practical Approach*. Alexandria, VA: United Way of America, 1996.

Tool Kit E

Data Preparation, Coding, and Processing

Preparing the Data

Preparing the data has two steps: cleaning the data and assigning identification tags. Cleaning data refers to looking at each completed data-collection form and removing any forms whose answers do not follow the directions or make no sense. These forms should be marked as to the reason they are not being used and then stored; you may want to review them at a later time when you are considering changes to the forms.

The next step is to assign an identification number to each respondent. The idea is to link the participant to the form and to any information gathered earlier or in the future; you will use the same ID each time the person is surveyed, interviewed, and so on. A simple way to do this is to give each respondent a sequential number starting with one through the last relevant number, being careful to avoid any duplication. In a program with fifty participants, they would be numbered one through fifty. A file of names with their corresponding numbers is then kept for future use. Only the ID number stays on the completed form, so that few people know the identity of the respondent. If you do not want to keep names at all, you must assign a different type of unique ID that the participant can use in the future and that will allow you to link all information about that person together. For example, you might ask people for the month of their birthday, the last letter of their first name, and the second digit of their social security number.[1] That combination of letters and numbers is their personal ID, one that they should be able to give each time (as long as you ask for the same pieces of information in the same order).

Coding the Data

Coding the questions is the next part of the process. A code number must be assigned to each possible answer for each question on the data collection instrument. Coding enables the person entering the data into a spreadsheet or database to type in only the number corresponding to an answer. Coding quantitative or closed-ended questions with a predetermined number of possible responses is the simplest. For yes-no answers, for example, "yes" might be represented by a "1" and "no" by a "2." For questions whose answer is a number, such as "How many times did you use the genealogy resources?" the numerical answer is also the code number. For questions whose answer is a ranking on a scale from one to five, those ranking numbers are the codes. Consistency in the codes assigned for "yes" and "no," for "not applicable," and for answers left blank will make both the coding and data entry easier. Once all the answers are assigned code numbers, you create a codebook, which is a directory for your data and includes the codes and where each piece of data is stored in the data file. (For more materials on coding, see Additional Resources: Data Collection and Analysis.)

Qualitative data are narrative or textual responses, rather than numerical ones, and they also need to be coded. Examples of qualitative data are responses to open-ended questions on tests and surveys or in interviews; essay answers on tests; self-report products such as journals; staff logs; observer notes; and survey respondents' comments under "Other." The process of coding qualitative data is similar to indexing a book. You must reduce the amount of text and organize the responses by patterns or trends. This activity is called content analysis and it enables you to convert pages of words to a finite number of response categories that can then be quantified.

The simplest method is to collate all the responses to a single question by cutting and pasting, manually or with software. Then read all the answers to a question, looking for patterns. As you read, note the themes. For example, in the comment section of a customer service survey, if more than one participant mentioned schedule as an issue and a number of participants wrote about transportation problems, "schedule" and "transportation" may be themes. Using these themes as response categories, assign each a code number or an abbreviated title. You might use SCHED for all answers that mentioned scheduling and TRAN for all answers with the theme of transportation. You can now reread all the responses, counting the number of respondents who gave a certain category as their answer. In many cases, a respondent's answer will include more than one theme and will have more than one code attached. Each code will be counted as a separate instance, even though the answers all came from the same respondent to a single question.

When you total the number of times each theme was mentioned, you can calculate the percentage of people who gave a certain response. In other words, you can now treat the textual responses almost as you would quantitative data. Of course, the code or label is not enough information for others; when you describe these results, you will need to write a composite response or a short paragraph summary that reflects the contents of them all.

Because content analysis is subjective, you may want to ask other staff members to verify the content analysis by reading the text with the codes in hand. Or have two people do the analysis and then compare and perhaps combine their results. Getting more people involved not only prevents bias, but also allows for more buy-in of the outcome measurement process.

Keep in mind that content analysis is easier using predetermined categories rather than having to search for emergent ones. So the second time you analyze qualitative data for the same program, the coding will be much simpler.

Processing the Data

Processing the data refers to entering the data code for each answer from each data collection instrument into a database—carefully and consistently—so that it can be stored, updated, and retrieved for data analysis. The database, depending on the number of respondents you have, may be created with paper and pencil or by using computer software programs. Many of the database and spreadsheet programs that can be used for data management and analysis are commonly owned by libraries already.[2] Spreadsheet programs (such as Excel) are easy to use for data entry and basic data analysis, such as frequencies and cross-tabulations, if your numbers are not too large. They also have excellent graphing and charting features, allowing you to create figures that can then be exported to a word processor for text reports. Databases (such as Access) are excellent for data entry and can generate text reports, but have limited analysis capabilities. More sophisticated and difficult (and expensive) statistical analysis software programs (such as SPSS) are also available. But you most probably do not need high-level statistical analysis.

Before the data are manipulated in any way, you must check for errors in the data entry. Otherwise you may be analyzing, interpreting, and reporting incorrect information that may form the basis of future program decisions. One way to check is to "eyeball" the data file for obvious errors and then, if there do not seem to be any, have a second person read 10 percent of the forms comparing them to the data files. A more stringent method is to have the second person enter 10 percent of the data into a separate file which is then compared to the first file. With either method, if there are only a few discrepancies, they can be discussed and corrected. If, however, many errors—or systematic problems—emerge, 100 percent of the data should be reentered.

NOTES

1. Marc Bolan, Kimberly Francis, and Jane Reisman, *How to Manage and Analyze Data for Outcome-Based Evaluation* (Seattle, WA: Evaluation Forum, 2000).
2. The United Way keeps a list of outcome measurement data management and analysis software programs and updates it annually. See http://national.unitedway.org/outcomes/resources/data_management_systems.cfm.

SOURCES

Abravanel, Martin D. *Surveying Clients about Outcomes*. Washington, DC: Urban Institute, 2003.

Bolan, Marc, Kimberly Francis, and Jane Reisman. *How to Manage and Analyze Data for Outcome-Based Evaluation*. Seattle, WA: Evaluation Forum, 2000.

Burroughs, Catherine M., and Fred B. Wood. *Measuring the Difference*. Seattle, WA: National Network of Libraries of Medicine, Pacific Northwest Region, 2000.

Durrance, Joan, and Karen E. Fisher. *How Libraries and Librarians Help: Outcome Evaluation Toolkit*. 2002. http://ibec.ischool.washington.edu.

Mika, Kristine L. *Program Outcome Evaluation*. Milwaukee, WI: Families International, 1996.

Project STAR for the Corporation for National Service. *Beginning with the End in Mind*. May 2004. http://projectstar.org/star/AmeriCorps.pmtoolkit.htm.

Taylor-Powell, Ellen, and others. *Analyzing Qualitative Data*. Madison: University of Wisconsin Extension, 1996.

United Way. *Measuring Program Outcomes: A Practical Approach*. Alexandria, VA: United Way of America, 1996.

Wholey, Joseph S. and others. *Handbook of Practical Program Evaluation*. San Francisco: Jossey-Bass, 1994.

Tool Kit F

Sampling

You will get the most complete assessment of your program if you measure outcomes for all of the participants in the program. However, if that is not possible, a sample (or portion of the participant population) should be used. Keep in mind that findings from a small sample of people with a high (over 50 percent) rate of response are far better (i.e., more valid) than findings from a larger number of people with a poor response rate. If your participant population is so large you need to sample, you probably should get assistance from a statistician, research firm, or university. Here, though, are some basics on sampling.

If the population you are surveying numbers less than 100, include them all or at least 80 percent of them. If the population is over 100, consider using a sample. For a population group (i.e., program participants or service users) of 100, you need to sample 80 people to ensure that 95 percent of the time the sample represents the population. For a group of 500, you need 217 responses. For a group of 1,000 people, you need 278 responses. As you can see, as the population size increases, the rate of increase in sample size decreases. Look up the number of people you will need to sample in a sample size table, available in many statistics and evaluation textbooks.

After the appropriate sample size is determined, you must increase that number by the estimated non-response rate. For example, if you want a sample of 100, you need to draw 100 names plus an additional number to cover the inevitable non-responders. Assuming a 50 percent response rate, you need to select an extra 50 names, for a total of 150.

Note that sampling is not just for surveys: it can also be used for pre- and posttesting; for selecting whose program records to use; and for deciding whom to interview.

The easiest way to draw a sample is by creating a list of all the individuals in your study's population, and then choosing one name or ID number by chance; for example, by closing your eyes and placing a finger on the list. After that, you select respondents at evenly spaced intervals (e.g., every fourth or twentieth person). You can select the interval by rolling dice or using that day's date. Once you have determined the first person to be surveyed, the rest of the list is automatically determined. This technique is called a "systematic random sample selection" and prevents a biased sample (i.e., choosing too many respondents with certain characteristics). Another easy way to draw a sample is to use a "simple random sample." This is like a lottery; you use a random number table from a statistics or evaluation textbook, a number from the random number generator feature on a calculator, or a randomized computer selection as you select each name.

Note that there are many other types of samples, such as stratified, cluster, mainstage, snowball, and quota samples. Don't panic—you don't need to know about any of these. Researchers doing scientific studies use such sophisticated sampling procedures to avoid errors that could affect the validity (accuracy of prediction to a larger population) and credibility (absence of bias) of their results. They also consider confidence intervals and probability calculations for their results. Since we don't plan to generalize to a universe of people, and plan to do only descriptive analysis of our results, we can happily put aside all these concerns.

SOURCES

Burroughs, Catherine M., and Fred B. Wood. *Measuring the Difference*. Seattle, WA: National Network of Libraries of Medicine, Pacific Northwest Region, 2000.

Taylor-Powell, Ellen. *Sampling*. Madison: University of Wisconsin Extension, 1998.

Urban Institute. *Surveying Clients about Outcomes*. Washington, DC: Urban Institute, 2003.

Glossary

Activities are functions of the library that are provided for and focused on users. Groupings of specific tasks that library staff members carry out comprise the activity. Activities can be subdivided into tasks and steps. Tasks are processes that convert inputs into output, and steps are sequential actions taken in the performance of a task. A library summer reading program, for example, is an activity that can be divided into a number of tasks (planning, publicity, implementation, etc.). Each of these tasks can be further divided into sequential steps. Steps for the task *publicity* might include (1) scheduling school visits; (2) scheduling PTA visits; (3) distributing posters to selected sites; (4) making presentations at schools and PTA meetings; and (5) publicizing the program in newspapers.

Anonymous responses are information that is collected from individuals without their names or identifiers so that no one, not even the evaluator, knows which results are from which participants.

Attitudes are an individual's personal views or feelings about an idea, issue, activity, or person. Attitudes are based on prior experience, affect current behavior, and tend to be unconscious and automatic. Attitudes include opinions and satisfaction assessments (e.g., "are you satisfied with the service you received at the library today?"). The intention or resolution to change a behavior is also considered an attitude.

Candidate outcomes are potential or proposed outcomes that must be verified before they are used. Usually the result of brainstorming and assumptions by library staff members, candidate outcomes must be checked with participants and others before being accepted as appropriate or correct measures of a program.

Coding is the assignment of a number to each possible answer to a question in order to ease data entry.

Community goals relate to the needs of the community and are beyond the scope of the library alone; the library's program is usually just one part of a larger effort to meet a community goal. (For example, to increase school readiness among elementary school children, decrease juvenile delinquency in teens, or increase socialization by isolated elders.) Note that *The New Planning for Results* does not use this term, but it is commonly used in outcome measurement. Answers the question: "What does the community hope to achieve in response to an identified community need?"

Condition. *See* status.

Confidential information is information that will not be shared with others. In evaluation, keeping information confidential usually means removing individuals' names and other identifiers from records so that results are not linked to any individual and only the evaluator knows who answered what. This guarantees the participants' privacy.

Content analysis is a process to organize text (qualitative data) into categories or themes so that it can be coded and analyzed.

Context is the amalgam of external influences on your program and its participants. Some examples are the social, political, and economic environment of the community in which your library functions, or the demands of an external funder. Context can also refer to aspects of the library environment in which your program is presented; these aspects include the library's service model, the attitudes and abilities of staff, and the attitudes and expectations of users.

Cross-tabulations are calculations that pull apart aggregated (grouped) data to let you look at them by characteristic or category. Cross-tabulations enable you to compare findings among subgroups of your participants to find a correlation between results and characteristics.

Data analysis is the process of calculation and cross-tabulation of data to provide meaningful information.

Data collection instruments are structured, standardized tools for gathering data. Examples include survey forms, interview forms, observation report forms, and tests.

Data collection methods include review of existing records, surveys, tests, interviews, observation, and self-reports.

Data entry. *See* data processing.

Data plan is a document summarizing the data collection and analysis decisions for each outcome indicator.

Data processing is the activity of entering, storing, updating, and retrieving information in a computer.

End outcome. *See* goals.

End user is the library customer or program participant who uses a service intended for him or her. Other users such as internal customers are not considered end users.

Evaluation is the measurement or verification of outcomes, using the indicators in relation to the selected standards of excellence. Evaluation data is usually collected through interviews, pre- and posttesting, professional observation, or self-administered surveys.

External communication is reporting results to individuals, groups, and agencies outside of the library, including the media.

Goals set the direction of a program, are developed in response to a demonstrated need, and are long range in nature. In both the *New Planning for Results* process and in outcome measurement, goals reflect the ultimate impacts desired for the users. In the *New Planning for Results*, goals relate to the library's mission statement. The goal is written from the user's perspective and is the ideal result of the selected service response. In outcome measurement, goals (also called end outcomes) relate directly to the community need and are always beyond the scope of the library alone to accomplish.

Immediate outcomes. *See* interim outcomes.

Impact is used as an example of measure 2 in *The New Planning for Results*: how well a service meets the needs of the people served. In this book, the terms *impact* and *outcome* are used synonymously. Note that often *outcome* refers to benefits to individual people, while *impact* refers to results at the community or policy level. When the term *impact* is used that way, the results are only visible after five to ten years. This is also sometimes called a societal outcome.

Indicators make the outcome tangible. They are the operational definitions of an outcome. Indicators are used to gauge success for the participant. They are measurable characteristics or behaviors that indicate achievement of the outcome. They demonstrate changes in knowledge, skills, behavior, attitude, or condition, or imply such changes. Note that the amount of expected change and the time frame are included in the indicator; for example, an increase in one reading level within one year; ability to use a database independently by December 1, 2006; successful completion of a sample citizenship exam at the end of the course). Answers the questions: "What does the user say or do that reveals the achievement of the intended outcome?" and "What will we measure that indicates the achievement?" Indicators may also be called change indicators or performance measures.

Initial outcomes. *See* interim outcomes.

Inputs are resources (such as money, staff, volunteers, facilities, collections, technology, community partners) used to plan and provide a program or service. Less visible inputs are the library's mission, service responses, and policies and procedures. Constraints on a program such as laws, regulations, and funding requirements are also inputs. Answers the question: "Which of our resources can we use to provide the service?"

Interim outcomes are milestones in the life of a project, events that are necessary for successful long-range outcomes. They are critical points at which project staff must decide whether to continue current activities or modify them in order to achieve the desired outcomes. Interim outcomes include short-term outcomes that are usually visible within the first year of a program; and intermediate outcomes that are usually not measurable until one to two years after the beginning of a program. Interim outcomes may also be called initial, short-term, or intermediate outcomes. Answers the questions: "What is the short-term benefit to the user from the program or service?" and "What will the user do that is necessary if he or she is to achieve the long-range outcome?"

Intermediate outcomes. *See* interim outcomes.

Internal communication is reporting results to people within the library, such as staff, volunteers, and board members.

Interpretation is the act of making sense of the data findings and drawing conclusions about them.

Logic model is a diagram or chart—like a flowchart—showing the assumptions (logic) behind your program and the relationships between your program activities and their outcomes. It shows the causal links between inputs, outputs, activities, outcomes, and a goal. A logic model may also be called a program model or outcome-sequence chart.

Long-range outcomes are key results for the end user that are typically visible and measurable only after a minimum of two years from the beginning of a program. These gains are complex, fundamental, and meaningful in the user's life. Long-range outcomes may also be called long-term or remote outcomes. *See also* outcomes.

Mean is the average of a series of scores or numbers, and is used as a statistical summary of data. To calculate the mean, add all the scores and divide the total by the number of responses.

Measures are tools to gauge the library's progress toward a goal. In *The New Planning for Results*, three types of measures are suggested. Measures one and three are output measures: number of people served and number of total units of service provided by the library. Measure two is an outcome measure: how well the service meets the needs of the people served.

Mode is the answer given most often by a group of participants, and is used as a statistical summary of data. To calculate the mode, count how many participants gave each response.

Objectives are traditionally projections of the amount of outputs to be delivered in a specified timeframe, with a standard of success. In *The New Planning for Results*, an objective can be a projection of any of three measures—output or outcome—with a standard of success and a date or time frame. In outcome measurement, objectives are usually called outcome measure statements. *See also* outcome statement.

Outcome management is a synonym for outcome measurement or outcome-based evaluation. It reflects an emphasis on the planning rather than the evaluation aspects of the approach.

Outcome measurement is a user-centered approach to the planning and assessment of programs or services that are provided to address particular user needs and are designed to achieve change for the user. Outcome measurement is used to assess the effectiveness or impact of a program. It is usually considered a form of qualitative evaluation. Outcome measurement may also be called outcome evaluation, outcome-based evaluation, outcome assessment, person-referenced value assessment, or results-based evaluation.

Outcome measurement plan is a plan consisting of a goal; a description of whom the program expects to affect; inputs; services or programs; outputs; outcomes; indicators; standards of success; and a data collection plan for the entire program. When presented as a diagram, such a plan is called a logic model.

Outcome statement is the outcome measurement equivalent of an objective. It explains what you expect to happen to a specified number or proportion of your users, as a result of your program, within a specified amount of time. The statement has five components: the user, an indicator verb (or measurable action), a quantity of the action, the percentage of users who will demonstrate the indicator, and a timeframe. For example, "By the end of the year, 90 percent of family literacy program participants (100) will double the amount of time they spend reading to their children each week."

Outcomes are benefits to the end user that demonstrate the effectiveness of a program or service. The benefits usually are changes in user knowledge, skills, behavior, attitude, or condition that may not have happened without the program or service. Benefits are also called consequences, achievements, impacts, or results. Answers the question: "What difference did our program make to the participant?"

Outputs are units of service resulting from the inputs and activities of the library. They reflect the volume of successful activities or products. Outputs are objectively quantified measures (such as number of books circulated, number of hours devoted to homework assistance, or number of attendees at an author reading). Note that in the design stage of *The New Planning for Results*, measure three is an output measure. In traditional evaluation, projected outputs with a timeline attached are referred to as objectives. Answers the question: "How much did the library do?"

Participants are the end users of a program. For example, adult learners are the participants in a literacy program.

Percentages are statistical summaries of data that depict relative size or proportion. To calculate the percentage, divide the number of people whom you are considering by the total number of relevant people, multiply by 100, and add the percentage sign.

Pilot-test is like a dress rehearsal, in this case for implementation of the outcome measurement data collection and analysis.

Pretest/posttest is an instrument administered at two or more points before, during, and after a program in order to collect comparative information. This is also called repeated measure design.

Private information. *See* confidential information.

Program is a set of related activities with a common purpose, usually provided to a targeted audience—that is, a specific group of users who have a common need or a common demographic. A program usually has a defined end point, either a time frame or goal. Examples of programs include family literacy, senior Internet online classes, training in genealogy research, and health lecture series. *Compare to* service.

Proxy indicator is a substitute for an observable behavior; it is a behavior that implies the outcome rather than demonstrating it directly.

Proxy measure is a substitute for an interim outcome; often it is an output that is necessary for the user to achieve another interim outcome.

Qualitative data is experiential and is related to the quality or character of something. Qualitative data is in the form of words; for example, customer satisfaction interviews.

Quantitative data is numerical information relating to the quantity or frequency of something. Quantitative data is in the form of numbers; for example, circulation statistics.

Reliability is the dependability and consistency of a data collection instrument. This is an essential quality of a data collection instrument (e.g., an interview form). For example, an interview form is considered reliable if it has been shown to give consistent results even when used by more than one person or in more than one setting.

Repeated measure design is a data collection approach that uses a pre- and posttest.

Results are the consequences or effects of services. Results can refer to outputs (products) or outcomes (benefits).

Sample is a group of participants selected to be representative somehow of the whole. The sample may be selected randomly or by specific attribute.

Service is an ongoing series of activities provided to any and all users. Examples include reference, interlibrary loan, and Internet access. *Compare to* program.

Service responses are library service priorities. Thirteen of them are delineated in *The New Planning for Results*. They are defined as "what a library does for, or offers to, the public in an effort to meet a set of well-defined community needs." Service responses are selected in the design phase of the planning process, after community needs have been identified, and when a library is ready to write its mission, set its goals, and determine its activities. This is also the time when outcomes should be determined.

Short-term outcomes are the first interim outcomes that are tangible and measurable. They are usually visible within the first year of a program. *See also* interim outcomes.

Stakeholders are people with a vested interest in the library, including users, trustees, funders, and collaborating agencies. They are sometimes called influencers.

Standards are criteria of success. Outcome measurement uses two standards of success. The first one is the amount of change a user will show; this standard is incorporated into the indicator. The second standard is the expected proportion or amount of outcomes the library will see (e.g., 75 percent of participants report a specified effect six months after a program; 20 percent of attendees at resume-writing workshops report getting job interviews). This second standard is used to gauge the success of the library's program, not of the patron's behavior. Answers the question: "How will we know that our program is a success?"

Status is one of the areas of change that outcome measurement uses. It refers to a person's position or standing within a group and more broadly refers to quality of life concerns or circumstances. Examples are educational status (e.g., in school or not, high school graduate or not), employment status (e.g., employed or not, promoted or not), citizenship status, physical and emotional well-being, and personal circumstances. Status may also be called condition.

Validity is the accuracy of an instrument to measure what it is supposed to. This is an essential quality of a data collection instrument (e.g., an observation checklist, a survey) in order for it to have credibility. A checklist is valid if it has been shown to accurately measure the indicator you want to measure—and not some other indicator.

Selected Bibliography

Outcome Measurement

Abend, Jennifer, and Charles R. McClure. "Recent Views on Identifying Impacts from Public Libraries." *Public Library Quarterly* 17, no. 3 (1999): 361–90.

Association of Specialized and Cooperative Library Agencies. "Outcomes Evaluation Issue." *Interface* 24, no. 4 (Winter 2002): 1–11.

Bertot, John Carlo, and Charles R. McClure. "Outcomes Assessment in the Networked Environment: Research Questions, Issues, Considerations, and Moving Forward." *Library Trends* 51, no. 4 (Spring 2003): 590–613.

Bolan, Marc, Kimberly Francis, and Jane Reisman. *How to Manage and Analyze Data for Outcome-Based Evaluation*. Seattle, WA: Evaluation Forum, 2000.

Burroughs, Catherine M., and Fred B. Wood. *Measuring the Difference: Guide to Planning and Evaluating Health Information Outreach*. Seattle, WA: National Network of Libraries of Medicine, Pacific Northwest Region, 2000.

Clegg, Judith, Jane Reisman, and others. *Managing the Transition to Outcomes-Based Planning and Evaluation*. Seattle, WA: Evaluation Forum, 1998.

Dervin, Brenda, and Benson Fraser. *How Libraries Help*. Stockton, CA: University of the Pacific Press, 1985.

Dresang, Eliza T., and others. *Outcome-Based Planning and Evaluation for Dynamic Youth Services*. Chicago: American Library Association, forthcoming.

Durrance, Joan, and Karen E. Fisher. "Determining How Libraries and Librarians Help." *Library Trends* 51, no. 4 (Spring 2003): 541–70.

Durrance, Joan, and Karen E. Fisher. *How Libraries and Librarians Help: A Guide to Identifying User-Centered Outcomes*. Chicago: American Library Association, 2004.

———. *How Libraries and Librarians Help: Outcome Evaluation Toolkit*. 2002. http://ibec.ischool.washington.edu.

———. "Towards Developing Measures of the Impact of Library and Information Services." *Reference and User Services Quarterly* 42, no. 1 (Fall 2002): 43–53.

Fraser, B., and C. R. McClure. "Toward a Framework for Assessing Library and Institutional Outcomes." *Portal: Libraries and the Academy* 2, no. 4 (2002): 505–28.

Hatry, Harry P. Performance *Measurement: Getting Results*. Washington, DC: Urban Institute, 1999.

Hatry, Harry, and Linda Lampkin, eds. *Key Steps in Outcome Management*. Washington, DC: Urban Institute, 2003. (First in a series of six short guides on outcome measurement.)

Hernon, Peter, and Robert E. Dugan. *An Action Plan for Outcomes Assessment in Your Library*. Chicago: American Library Association, 2002.

———. "Outcomes Are Key but Not the Whole Story." *Journal of Academic Librarianship* 28, no. 1/2 (2002): 54–55.

Horn, Claudia B. *Outcome-Based Evaluation for Literacy Programs*. Syracuse, NY: Literacy Volunteers of America, 2001.

Innovation Network, Inc. Point K Learning Center. A suite of free online planning and evaluation tools that assist the user in writing an outcome-based evaluation plan. The tools include a Logic Model Builder, an Evaluation Plan Builder, and an Evaluation Survey Builder. http://www.innonet.org/tools.

Institute of Museum and Library Services. *New Directives, New Directions: Documenting Outcomes*. Washington, DC: Institute of Museum and Library Services, 2002. Also available at http:// www.imls.gov/grants/current/crnt_obebasics.htm.

———. *Perspectives on Outcome Based-Evaluation for Libraries and Museums*. Washington, DC: Institute of Museum and Library Services, 2000. Also available at http://www.imls.gov/pubs/pdf/pubobe.pdf.

W. K. Kellogg Foundation. *Evaluation Handbook*. Battle Creek, MI: W. K. Kellogg Foundation, 1998. (See especially pages 28–46 on outcome measurement.) Also available at http://www.wkkf.org/tools/evaluation/Pub770.pdf.

———. *Evaluation Toolkit*. http://www.wkkf.org/programming/extra.aspx. (A free web-based tutorial that takes the user to resources [including those below] via links.)

———. *Guiding Program Direction with Logic Models*. Battle Creek, MI: W. K. Kellogg Foundation, 2003. (Nine-page introduction to logic models.) Also available at http://www.wkkf.org/pubs/tools/evaluation/LMDG summary_00447_03674.pdf.

———. *Logic Model Development Guide: Using Logic Models to Bring Together Planning, Evaluation, and Action*. Battle Creek, MI: W. K. Kellogg Foundation, 2001. Also available at http://www.wkkf.org/pubs/tools/evaluation/Pub3669.pdf.

Kirkpatrick, D. L. "Evaluation of Training." In *Training and Development Handbook*, edited by R. L. Craig and L. R. Bittels, 135–60. New York: McGraw-Hill, 1967.

Lance, Keith Curry, and others. *Counting on Results: New Tools for Outcome-Based Evaluation of Public Libraries*. Final Report. Washington, DC: Institute of Museum and Library Services, 2002. Also available at http://www.lrs.org/CoR.asp.

Marshall, Joanne Gard. "Determining Our Worth, Communicating Our Value." *Library Journal* 125, no. 19 (November 15, 2000): 28–30.

McCraw, Cherie, and others. *LSTA Outcome-Based Evaluation Toolkit*. Tallahassee, FL: Florida Department of State, Division of Library and Information Services, 2004. Also available at http://www.lstatoolkit. com.

McNamara, Carter. *Basic Guide to Outcomes-Based Evaluation for Nonprofit Organizations with Very Limited Resources*. http://www.mapnp.org/library/evaluatn/outcomes.htm.

Mika, Kristine L. *Program Outcome Evaluation: A Step-by-Step Handbook*. Milwaukee, WI: Families International, 1996.

Morley, Elaine, and others. *A Look at Outcome Measurement in Nonprofit Agencies*. Washington, DC: Urban Institute, 2000.

———. *Outcome Measurement in Nonprofit Organizations: Current Practices and Recommendations*. Washington, DC: Independent Sector, 2001.

National Science Foundation. *Online Evaluation Resource Library*. http://www.oerl.sri.com.

Patton, Michael Quinn. *Utilization-Focused Evaluation*. 3rd ed. Thousand Oaks, CA: Sage, 1997. (See especially pages 147–77.)

Poll, Roswitha. "Measuring Impact and Outcome of Libraries." *Performance Measurement and Metrics* 4, no. 1 (2003): 5–12.

Project Literacy Victoria. *Outcome Measurement for a Community Literacy Program*. Victoria, BC: Project Literacy Victoria, 2001. Also available at http://www.plv.bc.ca/outcome/programoutcome.pdf.

Project STAR for the Corporation for National and Community Service. A number of performance measurement toolkits, one for each of AmeriCorps' programs. Includes an example of performance measurement of a literacy program. Start with *Beginning with the End in Mind: A Performance Measurement Toolkit for AmeriCorps*. May 2004. Available at http://www.projectstar.org/star/AmeriCorps.pmtoolkit.htm. See also the logic model worksheets at http://www.projectstar.org/star/logic_models.htm and http://www.projectstar.org/star/VISTA_PM_toolkit_11.03.04.pdf.

Reisman, Jane. *A Field Guide to Outcome-Based Program Evaluation*. Seattle, WA: Evaluation Forum, 1994.

Reisman, Jane, and Judith Clegg. *Outcomes for Success!* Seattle, WA: Evaluation Forum, 2000.

Rubin, Rhea Joyce. "Predicting Outcomes: Outcome Measures as a Planning Tool." In *How Libraries and Librarians Help: A Guide to Identifying User-Centered Outcomes*, by Joan Durrance and Karen E. Fisher, 84–93. Chicago: American Library Association, 2004.

Sadlon and Associates, Inc. *Workbook: Outcome Measurement of Library Programs*. Tallahassee: State Library of Florida, 2000. Also available at http://dlis.dos.state.fl.us/bld/research_office/outcomeeval.wkbk.doc.

Schalock, Robert L. *Outcome-Based Evaluation*. 2nd ed. New York: Kluwer / Plenum, 2001.

Steffen, Nicolle O., Keith Curry Lance, and Rochelle Logan. "Time to Tell the Whole Story: Outcome-Based Evaluation and the Counting on Results Project." *Public Libraries* 41, no. 4 (July–August 2002): 222–28.

———. "Who's Doing What: Outcome-Based Evaluation and Demographics for the Counting on Results Project." *Public Libraries* 41, no. 5 (September–October 2002): 271–79.

Taylor-Powell, Ellen, and others. *Planning a Program Evaluation*. Program Development and Evaluation, University of Wisconsin-Extension. (A series of short pamphlets, 1996–2002.) Also available at http://www.uwex.edu/ces/pdande/evaluation.

United Way. *Agency Experiences with Outcome Measurement: Survey Findings*. Alexandria, VA: United Way of America, 2000.

———. *Measuring Program Outcomes: A Practical Approach.* Alexandria, VA: United Way of America, 1996.

United Way Outcome Measurement Network. http:// national.unitedway.org/outcomes/.

University of Wisconsin-Extension. *Enhancing Program Performance with Logic Models.* 2002. http://www .uwex.edu/ces/lmcourse. (Free web-based course on logic models and outcome measurement.)

Usherwood, R. C. "Accounting for Outcomes: Demonstrating the Impact of Public Libraries." *Australasian Public Libraries and Information Services* 5, no. 1 (2002): 5–13.

Williams, Harold S., and others. *Outcome Funding: A New Approach to Targeted Grantmaking.* 3rd ed. Rensselaerville, NY: Rensselaerville Institute, 1995.

Additional Resources

Data Collection and Analysis

Abravanel, Martin D. *Surveying Clients about Outcomes.* Washington, DC: Urban Institute, 2003.

> A 52-page pamphlet in the excellent Series on Outcome Management for Non-Profit Organizations.

Bolan, Marc, Kimberly Francis, and Jane Reisman. *How to Manage and Analyze Data for Outcome-Based Evaluation.* Seattle, WA: Evaluation Forum, 2000.

> This clearly written book, which comes with a diskette of fictitious program data for practice purposes, describes how to manage program data with specifics on how to use Access and Excel for data preparation and analysis.

Bond, Sally, and Kathleen Rapp. *Taking Stock: A Practical Guide to Evaluating Your Own Programs.* Chapel Hill, NC: Horizon Research, 1997.

> Although this slim volume (93 pages) approaches evaluation from a traditional perspective, the sections on data collection are well presented for novices.

Conway, Michael J. *How to Collect Data.* Info-Line issue no. 0008. Alexandria, VA: American Society for Training and Development, 1998.

> An excellent 16-page introduction to data collection.

Fink, Arlene, and Jacqueline Kosecoff. *How to Conduct Surveys: A Step-by-Step Guide.* 2nd ed. Thousand Oaks, CA: Sage, 1998.

> A practical and concise (111 pages) paperback guide.

Fink, Arlene, and others. *The Survey Kit.* 10 vols. 2nd ed. Thousand Oaks, CA: Sage, 2002.

> If Fink's *How to Conduct Surveys* (above) is not enough for you, this newly updated ten-volume set should answer all your questions about written surveys and interviews. Each volume (100 to 200 pages) focuses on a specific subject: self-administered and mail surveys, in-person interviews, telephone interviews, sampling, reliability and validity, data analysis, and reports. The first two volumes, *The Survey Handbook* and *How to Ask Survey Questions*, are especially useful to new survey developers.

Glitz, Beryl. *Focus Groups for Libraries.* Chicago: Medical Library Association, 1999.

> The author writes for library managers who will be conducting focus groups using in-house staff. She gives practical advice on selecting a moderator, preparing the questions, moderating and recording the discussion, analyzing and reporting results, and using the findings. She also provides two case studies of focus group projects in libraries.

Gorman, G. E., and Peter Clayton. *Qualitative Research for the Information Professional: A Practical Handbook.* 2nd ed. New York and London: Facet, 2005.

> Two Australian professors of library and information science wrote this textbook and a companion volume on quantitative statistics for beginning researchers. Although the assumption is that the reader is interested in research fieldwork—as compared to practical study of a library program—the chapters on observation, interviewing, and group discussion techniques provide much useful and understandable information.

Hatry, Harry P., Jake Cowan, and Michael Hendricks. *Analyzing Outcome Information: Getting the Most from Data.* Washington, DC: Urban Institute, 2004.

> A very useful 33-page pamphlet in the excellent Series on Outcome Management for Non-Profit Organizations by Harry Hatry, the outcome measurement guru behind the United Way program.

Henerson, Marlene E., Lynn L. Morris, and Carol J. Fitz-Gibbon. *How to Measure Attitudes*. Newbury Park, CA: Sage, 1987.

> Attitudes, unlike skills or knowledge, cannot be observed directly; they are therefore more difficult to measure. This is an excellent guide to developing data collection instruments for measuring attitudes.

Herman, Joan, and others. *Program Evaluation Kit*. 9 vols. 2nd ed. Thousand Oaks, CA: Sage, 1987.

> A nine-volume set covering all facets of program evaluation. Each paperback volume is medium length (96 to 192 pages) on one of the following topics: how to focus an evaluation, how to design a program evaluation, how to use qualitative methods, how to assess program implementation, how to measure attitudes, how to measure performance tests, how to analyze data, how to communicate evaluation findings. Each volume can stand alone and may be purchased separately.

Krueger, Richard A., and David L. Morgan, eds. *The Focus Group Kit*. 6 vols. Thousand Oaks, CA: Sage, 1998.

> A six-volume set covering everything about focus groups. Each volume is a short (100 pages), clear paperback on one of the following focus group topics: planning, developing questions, involving community members, moderating, analyzing results, and reporting results. Each volume can stand alone and may be purchased separately.

Nayyar-Stone, Ritu, and Harry P. Hatry. *Finding Out What Happens to Former Clients*. Washington, DC: Urban Institute, 2003.

> A 32-page pamphlet in the excellent Series on Outcome Management for Non-Profit Organizations.

Niles, Robert. *Information about Statistics Every Writer Should Know*. http://nilesonline.com/stats.

> Useful layman's definitions and guidelines for explaining sampling and data analysis. Written for journalists.

Patton, Michael Quinn. *Utilization-Focused Evaluation*. 3rd ed. Thousand Oaks, CA: Sage, 1997.

> This highly respected and widely used textbook on program evaluation includes an excellent chapter on data collection methods (pages 239–64).

Peterson, Robert A. *Constructing Effective Questionnaires*. Thousand Oaks, CA: Sage, 1999.

> Another short (152 pages) manual for the new evaluator.

Pezzullo, John. *Web Pages That Perform Statistical Calculations*. http://www.statpages.net.

> Links to over 600 web pages that do calculations or offer other statistics resources.

Phillips, Patricia P., and others. *Evaluation Data: Planning and Use*. Info-Line issue no. 0304. Alexandria, VA: American Society for Training and Development, 2003.

> In a 16-page booklet, the authors present an eight-step evaluation approach. The second half of their model gives a quick bite of useful information on data collection for the new evaluator.

Project STAR for the Corporation for National Service. *Analyzing Performance Measurement Data*. http://www.projectstar.org/star/generic.usersguide.htm.

> Clear directions on how to do basic analysis. Exercises allow user to try each step on sample survey forms provided.

———. *Data Collection*. http://www.projectstar.org/star/generic/usersguide.htm.

> Clear, direct, six-step method for designing and testing a data collection plan.

Reisman, Jane. *A Field Guide to Outcome-Based Program Evaluation*. Seattle, WA: Evaluation Forum, 1994.

> After a 30-page introduction to outcome measurement concepts, the next 75 pages of this book introduce data methods with specifics on formats, sampling, and statistical analysis for novices.

Salkind, Neil J. *Statistics for People Who (Think They) Hate Statistics*. Thousand Oaks, CA: Sage, 2000.

> As the title suggests, an introduction to statistics for novices.

Simon, Judith Sharken. *Conducting Successful Focus Groups: How to Get the Information You Need to Make Smart Decisions*. St. Paul, MN: Amherst H. Wilder Foundation, 1999.

> A clear, concise, 67-page introduction to how and when to use focus groups.

Taylor-Powell, Ellen, and others for the University of Wisconsin-Extension. *Program Development and Evaluation*.

A series of excellent, short (2 to 67 pages) publications on data collection topics such as surveys, sampling, direct observation, questionnaire design, and analyzing quantitative and qualitative data. Available in print from the University of Wisconsin cooperative Extension Publications in Madison, Wisconsin, or under "Program Development and Evaluation" at the publications section of http://cecommerce.uwex.edu.

Wholey, Joseph S. , and others. *Handbook of Practical Program Evaluation*. San Francisco: Jossey-Bass, 1994.

A large (622 pages), broad textbook on evaluation that has excellent chapters on evaluation design, data collection and analysis, and effectiveness.

Zemke, Ron, and Thomas Kramlinger. *Figuring Things Out. Reading*, MA: Addison-Wesley, 1982.

Written for trainers, this book has strong introductions to focus groups, interviews, gathering information, surveys and questionnaires, and sampling. These sections are recommended despite the book's 1982 publication date.

Zweizig, Douglas, and others. *The Tell It! Manual: The Complete Program for Evaluating Library Performance*. Chicago: American Library Association, 1996.

Another book on a broader topic that includes excellent chapters on data collection methods. See part 3, which has nine chapters (111 pages) on surveying, interviewing, attitude measurement, and more.

Workforms

Program Suitability for Outcome Measurement

Directions

1. Enter the name and a brief description of the program.
2. Gather a group of people to discuss the program.
3. Discuss the following questions and decide if the answer is "yes" or "no." Place an X in the appropriate box for each question.
4. When you are finished with each section, total the number of "yes" answers in each section and record your answers on the subtotal line.
5. When you have completed all four sections record the subtotals for each section in the score box at the end of the form.
6. If 15 or more of the answers are "yes," your program is well suited for outcome measurement. If not, you should select a different program.

Program Name and Description

_____

_____

_____

Purpose and Design of Program

YES	NO	
		1. Has the program been developed in response to an identified need?
		2. Can this program have a significant (not total) influence on the need?
		3. Is impact on the end user a major purpose of the program?
		4. Is the program more concerned with impact than with outputs?
		5. Is it more concerned with public service than with internal library operations?
		6. Is the program focused on effectiveness rather than efficiency?
		7. Is it focused more on users' benefit than users' satisfaction?
		8. Does the program—or a user's participation in it—have a distinct beginning and end?
		Subtotal

Users

YES	NO	
		9. Are the users clearly defined?
		10. Do the users participate consistently so you can track their progress?
		11. Will users be willing to participate in an evaluation?
		Subtotal

(Cont.)

Impact

YES	NO	
		12. Is the desired impact measurable?
		13. Will the impact occur within a few years (so that it can be observed)?
		Subtotal

Management, Staff, and Stakeholders

YES	NO	
		14. Do the management and staff have a service or user orientation?
		15. Is the program stable enough to undertake this endeavor?
		16. Is there a library leadership commitment to devote resources to outcome measurement and then to act on the results?
		17. Are the program stakeholders supportive?
		18. Will measuring outcomes provide useful feedback to improve the program?
		19. Will measuring outcomes improve accountability to the library or stakeholders by demonstrating effectiveness?
		Subtotal

Score

YES	NO	SECTION
		Purpose and Design of Program
		Users
		Impact
		Management, Staff, and Stakeholders
		TOTAL

Prepared by: _____   Date: _____

Directions

1. Enter the name and a brief description of the program. (See Workform 1.)
2. List the candidate outcomes in the lines numbered 1, 2, 3, 4. (If you have more outcomes, add additional pages.)
3. Begin with the first candidate outcome.
   a. Draft an outcome with specific user + will + outcome verb + object.
   b. Complete the "if-then" statements.
4. Continue through the remaining candidate outcomes.

Program Name and Description

_____

_____

_____

1. Candidate Outcome: _____

   1A. Draft outcome: _____

_____

   1B. If-Then Statements

      If the library does _____,

      then participants will _____.

      If participants _____,

      then they will _____.

      If participants_____,

      then they will _____.

      If participants _____,

      then they will _____.

2. Candidate Outcome: _____

   2A. Draft outcome: _____

_____

   2B. If-Then Statements

      If the library does _____,

      then participants will _____.

      If participants _____,

      then they will _____.

(Cont.)

2B. If-Then Statements (*Cont.*)

If participants _____,

then they will _____.

If participants _____,

then they will _____.

3. Candidate Outcome: _____

3A. Draft outcome: _____

_____

3B. If-Then Statements

If the library does _____,

then participants will _____.

If participants _____,

then they will _____.

If participants _____,

then they will _____.

If participants _____,

then they will _____.

4. Candidate Outcome: _____

4A. Draft outcome: _____

_____

4B. If-Then Statements

If the library does _____,

then participants will _____.

If participants _____,

then they will _____.

If participants _____,

then they will _____.

If participants _____,

then they will _____.

Prepared by: _____   Date: _____

Directions

1. Enter the program name and description from Workform 2.
2. Select a candidate outcome from Workform 2 that stood up to the If-Then Exercise.
3. Evaluate the candidate outcome using the criteria listed.
   a. Place an X in the "Yes" box if the statement meets the criterion.

   b. Place an X in the "No" box if the statement does not meet the criterion.
4. If the candidate outcome does not meet at least four out of the six criteria, revise the statement or return to Workform 2 to identify an interim or long-term outcome that will meet the criteria.
5. Repeat this exercise for all of the candidate outcomes on Workform 2.

Program Name and Description

_____

_____

_____

Candidate Outcome

_____

_____

_____

YES	NO	CRITERIA
		1. Is the outcome connected logically to the program goal and activities?
		2. Is the outcome valuable for the participants?
		3. Is the outcome important to the library?
		4. Is the outcome achievable by the program?
		5. Is the outcome compelling to stakeholders?
		6. Is the outcome culturally and contextually sensitive?

Candidate Outcome

_____

_____

YES	NO	CRITERIA
		1. Is the outcome connected logically to the program goal and activities?
		2. Is the outcome valuable for the participants?
		3. Is the outcome important to the library?
		4. Is the outcome achievable by the program?
		5. Is the outcome compelling to stakeholders?
		6. Is the outcome culturally and contextually sensitive?

(Cont.)

Candidate Outcome

_____

_____

_____

YES	NO	CRITERIA
		1. Is the outcome connected logically to the program goal and activities?
		2. Is the outcome valuable for the participants?
		3. Is the outcome important to the library?
		4. Is the outcome achievable by the program?
		5. Is the outcome compelling to stakeholders?
		6. Is the outcome culturally and contextually sensitive?

Candidate Outcome

_____

_____

_____

YES	NO	CRITERIA
		1. Is the outcome connected logically to the program goal and activities?
		2. Is the outcome valuable for the participants?
		3. Is the outcome important to the library?
		4. Is the outcome achievable by the program?
		5. Is the outcome compelling to stakeholders?
		6. Is the outcome culturally and contextually sensitive?

Prepared by: _____   Date: _____

Directions

1. Complete a copy of Workform 4 for each outcome you identified on Workform 3.
2. Enter the program name and description from Workform 3.
3. Enter an outcome from Workform 3 that met at least four of the six criteria.

PART A

1. Answer questions 1–4. If the "So what?" response has not brought you to an obvious end outcome, continue asking and answering that question.

2. Select one or more interim outcome(s) from 1, 2, or 3. Remember that immediate outcomes should be visible by the end of the first year of your program, and that intermediate outcomes should be visible within three years. Write the selected interim outcomes in part B.
3. Select a long-range outcome from 3 or 4. Remember that long-range outcomes usually take more than three years to be measurable. The long-range outcome may be the end outcome (very close to the community goal) or it may be closer to an intermediate outcome. Write the selected long-range outcome in part B.

Program Name and Description

_____

_____

_____

Outcome

_____

_____

_____

PART A

1. The user does/feels/knows _____

_____

So what? _____

_____

2. The user does/feels/knows _____

_____

So what? _____

_____

3. The user does/feels/knows _____

_____

So what? _____

_____

(Cont.)

PART A *(Cont.)*

4. The user does/feels/knows _____

_____

So what? _____

_____

PART B

Selected Interim Outcome: _____

_____

_____

Selected Interim Outcome 2: _____

_____

_____

Selected Long-Range Outcome: _____

_____

_____

Prepared by: _____   Date: _____

Directions

1. Enter the program name and description from Workform 4.
2. List the potential users of this program on line 1.
3. List the user needs being addressed in this program on line 2.
4. Describe the activities you will offer to support the program on line 3.
5. Identify the inputs (resources such as money, staff, volunteers, facilities, collections, technology, community partners, etc.) that will be allocated to support the program activities on line 4.

6. Identify the outputs (units of service resulting from the inputs, such as the number of books circulated, the number of staff or volunteer hours devoted to homework assistance, or the number of attendees at an author reading) on line 5.
7. List the interim outcomes from all of the copies of Workform 4 that you completed for this program on line 6.
8. List the long-range outcomes from all of the copies of Workform 4 that you completed for this program on line 7.

Program Name and Description

_____

_____

_____

1. The *Potential Users* are:

_____

_____

_____

_____

_____

2. We will address this identified *User Need*:

_____

_____

_____

_____

_____

3. In order to meet the need, we will provide these *Program Activities*:

_____

_____

_____

_____

_____

(Cont.)

4. In order to present the program, we will use the following *Inputs*:

_____

_____

_____

_____

_____

5. During the program cycle, we will produce the following *Outputs*:

_____

_____

_____

_____

_____

6. The users will manifest the following *Interim Outcome(s)* during the program cycle:

_____

_____

_____

_____

_____

7. The users will demonstrate these *Long-Range Outcome(s)* at the end or after the program cycle:

_____

_____

_____

_____

_____

Prepared by: _____   Date: _____

Directions

1. Complete a copy of this workform for each outcome listed in part B of Workform 4.
2. Select one of the outcomes from Part B of Workform 4 and write it on the outcome line.
3. Complete parts A and B of the workform.

PART A

1. List the indicators for the outcome in part A of the workform on the lines labeled Draft Indicator. There are places for three indicators on the form. If you have more than three indicators, use a second copy of the form.

2. Start with your first indicator.
   a. Answer each question in the table.
   b. If you cannot answer all of the questions positively for the indicator, you must revise that indicator.
   c. When you have finished your review of the indicator and made all necessary revisions, write the final indicator on the appropriate line in part B of this workform.
3. Continue the process with your second and third indicators.
4. When you have completed part A of the workform, you should have a group of indicators, each of which matches all eight of the criteria.

Outcome: _____

_____

_____

PART A: Review of Individual Indicators

Draft Indicator 1: _____

_____

YES	NO	
		1. Is the indicator specific and unambiguous?
		2. Is the indicator observable and concrete?
		3. Is the indicator measurable?
		4. Is the indicator time-bound?
		5. Is the indicator unique/different from the other indicators?
		6. Is the indicator understandable by staff and stakeholders?
		7. Is the indicator culturally appropriate?
		8. Does the indicator include the amount required for success?

(Cont.)

PART A: Review of Individual Indicators *(Cont.)*

Draft Indicator 2: _____

_____

YES	NO	
		1. Is the indicator specific and unambiguous?
		2. Is the indicator observable and concrete?
		3. Is the indicator measurable?
		4. Is the indicator time-bound?
		5. Is the indicator unique/different from the other indicators?
		6. Is the indicator understandable by staff and stakeholders?
		7. Is the indicator culturally appropriate?
		8. Does the indicator include the amount required for success?

Draft Indicator 3: _____

_____

YES	NO	
		1. Is the indicator specific and unambiguous?
		2. Is the indicator observable and concrete?
		3. Is the indicator measurable?
		4. Is the indicator time-bound?
		5. Is the indicator unique/different from the other indicators?
		6. Is the indicator understandable by staff and stakeholders?
		7. Is the indicator culturally appropriate?
		8. Does the indicator include the amount required for success?

(Cont.)

Directions

PART B

1. Review all the final indicators below and answer the questions in the table.
2. If you answer "yes" to all three questions, you have completed the process of developing indicators for this outcome.

3. If you answer "no" to any of the three questions, you will need to revise your final indicators again or develop one or more additional indicators for this outcome.
4. Use another copy of this workform to review your new or revised draft indicators.

PART B: Review of All Indicators

Final Indicator 1: _____

_____

Final Indicator 2: _____

_____

Final Indicator 3: _____

_____

YES	NO	
		1. Taken as a whole, do the indicators demonstrate the outcomes?
		2. Taken as a whole, do the indicators provide multiple perspectives on the outcome?
		3. Do the indicators in conjunction with the outcome tell a story?

Prepared by: _____   Date: _____

Directions

1. Complete a copy of Workform 7 for each of the indicators in part B of each of the copies of Workform 6 that you completed.
2. Copy the "Outcome" information from Workform 6 to line 1.
3. Indicate if this is an interim or long-range outcome by placing a check in the appropriate box on lines 1a or 1b.
4. Describe the participants in your program on line 2.

5. List one of the final indicators for this outcome from part B of Workform 6 on line 3.
6. Define the standard of success for each participant (line 2) for this indicator on line 4.
7. Define the quantity and percentage of the specified people (line 4) who will demonstrate the indicator on line 5.
8. Identify the date by which the standard of program success (line 5) will be achieved on line 6.

1. Outcome or benefit:

_____

_____

_____

    1a. _____ This is an interim outcome.   1b. _____ This is a long-range outcome.

2. Who will achieve the outcome?

_____

_____

_____

3. What behavior/action will show us that the outcome is achieved? (Indicator):

_____

_____

_____

4. Quantity of action? (Standard of success for participant):

_____

_____

_____

5. Quantity and percentage of the specified people who will demonstrate the indicator? (Standard of success for program):

_____

_____

_____

6. During what time period/By when? (Time frame):

_____

_____

Prepared by: _____   Date: _____

Directions

1. Complete a copy of this workform for each indicator listed on part B of Workform 6.
2. Enter the outcome from Workform 6 on the appropriate line.
3. Enter one of the indicators for that outcome on the next line.

PART A

1. Answer the questions in each of the six tables that represent common data collection methods.
2. Identify the two or three data collection methods that received the most "yes" responses, and use those data collection methods as the bases for answering the questions in part B.

PART A: Review of Data Collection Methods

Outcome: _____

Indicator: _____

YES	NO	REVIEW OF EXISTING RECORDS
		1. Do existing records already track this indicator?
		2. Can you get access to them?
		3. Are they kept consistently?
		4. Will you be able to get permission to use them?

YES	NO	SURVEYS
		1. Will participants be able to understand a written form?
		2. Will they be able to respond in writing?
		3. Will they be willing to answer your questions honestly?
		4. Will they be able to answer accurately?

YES	NO	TESTS
		1. Are you measuring changes in skill or knowledge?
		2. Are there existing tests you can use?
		3. Will participants be willing to take the test?
		4. Will they be able to take a test orally or in writing?

YES	NO	INTERVIEWS
		1. Do you need information from the participants' perspective?
		2. Do you need to ask open-ended questions?
		3. Will participants be willing to be interviewed?
		4. Will participants be able to respond to an interviewer?

(Cont.)

PART A: Review of Data Collection Methods (Cont.)

YES	NO	OBSERVATION
		1. Are you measuring an observable skill or behavior?
		2. Will there be an opportunity for observation?
		3. Will the participants feel comfortable being observed?
		4. If not, can someone observe covertly?

YES	NO	SELF-REPORTS
		1. Do journal or other written assignments fit your program?
		2. Will the participants be willing to self-report?
		3. Will they be able to self-report?
		4. Will you be able to get the information you need from their reports?

PART B

Directions

1. Enter the two or three data collection methods that received the most "yes" answers in part A on the "Possible Data Collection" lines.
2. For each selected method, answer the questions in the table.

3. Select the method that meets the most criteria and enter on the "Selected Data Collection Method" line.

Possible Data Collection Method 1: _____

YES	NO	PRACTICALITIES
		1. Is this method as direct as possible?
		2. Does your program have the necessary expertise?
		3. If not, can you find or hire experts?
		4. Is the method culturally sensitive to the participants?
		5. Is the method timely?
		6. Can you find the staff time?
		7. Can your budget afford the other costs?

(Cont.)

PART B (*Cont.*)

Possible Data Collection Method 2: _____

_____

YES	NO	PRACTICALITIES
		1. Is this method as direct as possible?
		2. Does your program have the necessary expertise?
		3. If not, can you find or hire experts?
		4. Is the method culturally sensitive to the participants?
		5. Is the method timely?
		6. Can you find the staff time?
		7. Can your budget afford the other costs?

Possible Data Collection Method 3: _____

_____

YES	NO	PRACTICALITIES
		1. Is this method as direct as possible?
		2. Does your program have the necessary expertise?
		3. If not, can you find or hire experts?
		4. Is the method culturally sensitive to the participants?
		5. Is the method timely?
		6. Can you find the staff time?
		7. Can your budget afford the other costs?

Selected Data Collection Method: _____

_____

This workform is adapted from one in *Evaluation Toolkit: Project Star,*
http://www.projectstar.org/star/VISTA_PM/toolkit_11.03.04.pdf.

Prepared by: _____   Date: _____

Relevance of Questions in a Data Collection Instrument

Directions

1. Complete one copy of this workform for each outcome.
2. List the outcome and data instruments being reviewed on the appropriate lines.
3. List the indicators for that outcome in column A.
3. List the information needed to measure your progress toward meeting each indicator in column B.
4. List the number of the question or questions from the data instruments under review that will collect the information identified in column B in column C.

5. When you have completed the form, check to be sure that there are questions in your data collection instrument to collect all needed information, and that every question in the instrument is related to a specific piece of information you need to measure progress toward one or more of your indicators.

Outcome: _____

_____

Data Instruments: _____

_____

A. INDICATOR	B. INFORMATION NEEDED	C. QUESTION NUMBER(S)

Prepared by: _____   Date: _____

Directions

1. Complete one copy of this workform for each outcome.
2. Write the outcome on the appropriate line.
3. Write the indicators for the outcome on the lines A and B. There are spaces for two indicators on this work-

form. If you have more than two indicators for this outcome, use a second copy of the workform.
4. Complete lines 1 through 8 for each indicator.

Outcome: _____

_____

A. Indicator 1: _____

_____

1. Data manager: _____

2. Data collection method(s): _____

_____

_____

3. Participants

    3a. Which participants will be included in the study? _____

    _____

    3b. How many participants will be studied? _____

    3c. If you will use a sample, how will it be selected? _____

    _____

4. Data collection process

    4a. Data collection supervisor: _____

    4b. Data collector(s): _____

    4c. Data collection location (e.g., on-site, by phone, by mail): _____

    _____

    4d. Data collection schedule (e.g., before workshop and at end; at registration and one month after close of program): _____

    4e. Data collection procedures (e.g., how many attempts to reach the participant; how to ensure a good response rate): _____

    _____

    _____

    _____

    _____

    4f. Date data collection ends: _____

(Cont.)

A. Indicator 1 (*Cont.*)

5. Data preparation

   5a. Person responsible: _____

   5b. Data cleaning schedule: _____

   _____

   5c. Process for creating identification tags: _____

   _____

   _____

   5d. ID tagging schedule: _____

   _____

   5e. Quality control: _____

   _____

   _____

   5f. Date data preparation is completed: _____

6. Data coding

   6a. Person responsible: _____

   6b. Notes on coding quantitative data: _____

   _____

   _____

   6c. Notes on coding qualitative data: _____

   _____

   _____

   6d. Quality control: _____

   _____

   _____

   _____

   6e. Date coding is completed: _____

7. Data processing

   7a. Person responsible: _____

   7b. Data entry schedule: _____

   7c. Quality control: _____

   _____

   _____

   7d. Date data processing is completed: _____

(*Cont.*)

A. Indicator 1 (*Cont.*)

8. Data analysis

8a. Data analyst: _____

8b. Types of analysis: _____

_____

_____

_____

_____

8c. Date data analysis is completed: _____

B. Indicator 2: _____

_____

1. Data manager: _____

2. Data collection method(s): _____

_____

_____

3. Participants

3a. Which participants will be included in the study? _____

_____

3b. How many participants will be studied? _____

3c. If you will use a sample, how will it be selected? _____

_____

4. Data collection process

4a. Data collection supervisor: _____

4b. Data collector(s): _____

4c. Data collection location (e.g., on-site, by phone, by mail): _____

_____

4d. Data collection schedule (e.g., before workshop and at end; at registration and one month after close of program): _____

_____

4e. Data collection procedures (e.g., how many attempts to reach the participant; how to ensure a good response rate): _____

_____

4f. Date data collection ends: _____

(*Cont.*)

B. Indicator 2 (*Cont.*)

5. Data preparation

   5a. Person responsible: _____

   5b. Data cleaning schedule: _____

   _____

   5c. Process for creating identification tags: _____

   _____

   _____

   5d. ID tagging schedule: _____

   _____

   5e. Quality control: _____

   _____

   _____

   5f. Date data preparation is completed: _____

6. Data coding

   6a. Person responsible: _____

   6b. Notes on coding quantitative data: _____

   _____

   _____

   6c. Notes on coding qualitative data: _____

   _____

   _____

   6d. Quality control: _____

   _____

   _____

   6e. Date coding is completed: _____

7. Data processing

   7a. Person responsible: _____

   7b. Data entry schedule: _____

   7c. Quality control: _____

   _____

   _____

   7d. Date data processing is completed: _____

(*Cont.*)

B. Indicator 2 (*Cont.*)

  8. Data analysis

    8a. Data analyst: _____

    8b. Types of analysis: _____

        _____

        _____

        _____

        _____

    8c. Date data analysis is completed: _____

Prepared by: _____   Date: _____

Directions

1. The workform provides a place to summarize the decisions you made on Workform 5 Inputs, Outputs, and Outcomes; Workform 7 Outcome Statement or Objective; and Workform 10, Data Plan.
2. Use the data from Workform 5 to complete line A and lines 1–5.
3. Use the data from Workform 7 to complete lines 6–10.
4. Use the data from Workform 10 to complete lines 11–13.
5. Use the data from Workform 7 to complete lines 14–17.
6. Use the data from Workform 10 to complete lines 18–22.

Program Name and Description

_____

_____

_____

1. The *Potential Users* are:

_____

_____

_____

_____

_____

2. We will address this identified *User Need*:

_____

_____

_____

_____

_____

3. In order to meet the need, we will provide these *Program Activities*:

_____

_____

_____

_____

_____

(Cont.)

4. In order to present the program, we will use the following *Inputs*:

_____

_____

_____

_____

_____

5. During the program cycle, we will produce the following *Outputs*:

_____

_____

_____

_____

_____

6. The users will manifest the following *Interim Outcome(s)* during the program cycle:

_____

_____

_____

_____

_____

7. What behavior/action will show us that the outcome is achieved? (Indicator):

_____

_____

_____

8. Quantity of action? (Standard of success for participant):

_____

_____

_____

9. Quantity and percentage of the specified people who will demonstrate the indicator?
(Standard of success for program):

_____

_____

_____

(Cont.)

10. During what time period/ By when? (Time frame):

_____

_____

_____

11. Data collection method?

_____

_____

_____

12. Which participants? (Sample or all? How will sample be selected?):

_____

_____

_____

13. When? (Schedule of collection):

_____

_____

_____

14. The users will demonstrate these *Long-Range Outcome(s)* at the end or after the program cycle:

_____

_____

_____

_____

15. What behavior/action will tell us that the outcome is achieved? (Indicator):

_____

_____

_____

16. Quantity of action? (Standard of success for participant):

_____

_____

_____

(*Cont.*)

17. Quantity and percentage of the specified people who will demonstrate the indicator? (Standard of success for program):

_____

_____

_____

18. During what time period/ By when? (Time frame):

_____

_____

_____

19. Data collection method?

_____

_____

_____

20. Which participants? (Sample or all? How will sample be selected?):

_____

_____

_____

21. When? (Schedule of collection):

_____

_____

_____

22. What data analysis process will be used?

_____

_____

_____

Prepared by: _____   Date: _____

Directions

1. Write the outcome on the appropriate line.
2. The numbers of the steps for each task in this book are listed in column A.
3. Indicate who will be responsible for completing each step in column B.

4. If others will be assigned to work with the person responsible for completing the step, list them in column C.
5. List the date by which the step is to be completed in column D.

Outcome: _____

_____

A. TASK/STEP	B. PERSON RESPONSIBLE	C. PERSON(S) ASSISTING	D. DEADLINE
2.1			
2.2			
2.3			
2.4			
3.1			
3.2			
3.3			
4.1			
4.2			
4.3			
4.4			
4.5			
5.1			
5.2			
5.3			
5.4			
5.5			
6.1			
6.2			
6.3			

Prepared by: _____   Date: _____

Directions

1. Enter the name and description of the program on the appropriate line.
2. Enter the individuals, organizations, or groups that will need or want information about the results of your program in column A.
3. Determine what each individual, organization, or group listed in column A will want to know and enter that in column B.
4. What will they be doing with the information? What would you like them to do with it? Enter that in column C.
5. Identify the most effective communication channels for each individual, organization, or group and enter them in column D.

Program Name and Description

_____

_____

_____

A. WHO WANTS/ NEEDS TO KNOW?	B. WHAT DO THEY WANT TO KNOW?	C. HOW WILL THEY USE IT?	D. COMMUNICATION CHANNEL(S)

Prepared by: _____   Date: _____

Directions

1. Write the name and description of the program under review in the appropriate line.
2. Review each of the elements in column A.
3. Indicate if the element has been considered for modifications by checking the appropriate box in column B.

4. If you check the "Yes" box in column B, describe the changes that are being proposed in column C.

Program Name and Description

_____

_____

_____

A. ELEMENT	B. MODIFICATION?		C. PROPOSED MODIFICATIONS
	YES	NO	
The outcome selected			
The indicator selected			
The target level			
A program activity			
Delivery strategy for an activity			
Program policies			
Program participation criteria			
Data collection method			
Data collection instrument			
Data collection timetable			
Data analysis types			
Data analysis software			
Data interpretation			
Staff and volunteer recruitment			
Staff training			
Collaborating agencies and organizations			
Public relations			
Resource (re)allocation			
Fund-raising			
Reporting methods or schedule			

Prepared by: _____   Date: _____

Index

RHEA JOYCE RUBIN is an independent library consultant specializing in planning and evaluation of library services, and training in related areas. She has been a *Planning for Results* trainer and coach to libraries across the United States and currently serves as the outcome measurement consultant for the California State Library, the Massachusetts Board of Library Commissioners, and the Connecticut State Library. A prolific author, Rubin has written eleven other published books and many journal articles, bibliographies, and contributions to books. She earned her MLS at the University of Wisconsin–Madison in 1973.